MAKI1
OF THE BIBLE

Helen-Ann Hartley

First published in Great Britain in 2011

Society for Promoting Christian Knowledge
36 Causton Street
London SW1P 4ST
www.spckpublishing.co.uk

British Library Cataloguing-in-Publication Data
A catalogue record for this book is available from the British Library

ISBN 978–0–281–06405–2

1 3 5 7 9 10 8 6 4 2

Typeset by Graphicraft Ltd, Hong Kong
Manufacture managed by Jellyfish
Printed in Great Britain by CPI Group

Produced on paper from sustainable forests

To all those who have inspired my love of the Bible,
and to the people and clergy of the Dioceses of Harare,
Zimbabwe and Christchurch, Aotearoa New Zealand

Contents

About the author

Helen-Ann Hartley is Director of Biblical Studies and Lecturer in New Testament at Ripon College Cuddesdon. She is Assistant Priest in the parish of Littlemore, Oxford and a member of the working group on Theological Education in the Anglican Communion.

Preface

The idea for this book came from the *Modern Church* group, and I am very grateful to its General Secretary, Jonathan Clatworthy, for all his encouragement with the project. Ruth McCurry at SPCK has been an outstanding and patient supporter, and I am most grateful to her careful reading of the text prior to publication. Much of this book was written while I was on sabbatical at the College of St John the Evangelist in Auckland, Aotearoa New Zealand, and the warm hospitality and welcome of the faculty, staff and students made my time all the more enriching. Many of the insights in this book derive from conversations and encounters that I had during my time there, and in particular, I would like to thank Jim White, Karena de Pont, Irene Ayalo, Megan Herles-Mooar, Patti Lao-Wood, Petra Barrie, Ellen Bernstein, Emily Colgan, Richard Bonifant, Hone Kaa and Christopher Douglas-Huriwai for their cheerful and often challenging words. Colleagues at Ripon College Cuddesdon looked after my teaching in my absence, and grateful thanks are due to Michael Lakey and Hywel Clifford, and to Martyn Percy for his encouragement to take up the sabbatical opportunity in the first place. I would also like to offer thanks to Harris Manchester College, Oxford, and in particular its Principal, Ralph Waller, for their hospitality and warmth in offering me use of their facilities. So many teachers and students of mine, past and present, have inspired my love of the Bible, and this book is, in part, dedicated to all of them. My first interest in the Bible, however, came from my parents, James and Patricia Francis, who taught me that any reading of the

Bible should be critical, creative and compassionate. I add to that list 'courageous', and I draw courage from my husband Myles, whose love and support are the foundations upon which I write. My link to Aotearoa New Zealand came through Jenny Te Paa, to whom I owe so much. Her words to me – to 'read widely, think deeply, and pray mightily' – resonate throughout my work, and I hope that the result is a fitting tribute to her tireless work for justice and theological education throughout the worldwide Anglican Communion.

Introduction

————◆●◆————

'Questions are the new Answers'
(advertisement, New York City, April 2010)

Every couple of months I contribute to my BBC local radio station's 'Friday Reflection'. Broadcast live just after the 6 a.m. news bulletin, it provides a few moments to pause in the midst of an otherwise fast-paced mix of presenter banter, music and the inevitable early morning travel and weather reports. Often the presenter emails me in advance, asking me if I'm doing anything interesting that he might mention to listeners (what clergy get up to is a source of never-ending interest). On this particular occasion, I reported that in the days following my broadcast I was to attend a family wedding in a Scottish castle, and deliver a lecture entitled 'Liberating Scripture' at a conference. I predicted that the castle event would invite some further enquiries once I was in the studio. I was wrong. The presenter announced the castle wedding to the listeners, and misread what I had typed about my latter engagement, informing everyone that I was to deliver a lecture on 'Liberating *Sculpture*'. Not surprisingly this caused hilarity; was I lecturing about emptying England's museums of overseas archaeological objects? I wasn't at all prepared for him then to ask me: 'So what's that about, then?' Being live radio, you don't get too much time to prepare your thoughts, so at 6.15 a.m. I said the 'h' word: 'hermeneutics'. 'Herma-*what*?' the presenter quipped. My answer? Simply that hermeneutics is about trying to understand what the Bible is saying, and that I wanted to encourage a

1

I wanted to encourage a conversational approach to reading the texts of the Bible

---

conversational approach to reading the texts of the Bible, with open hearts and open minds. Driving home, I reflected on this unexpected early morning encounter, realizing that it marked an important stage in my own understanding: a chance remark, a conversation, and, dare I say, an element of humour.[1]

This book is not intended to be a comprehensive overview of the formal academic attempt to make sense of the Bible (the history of biblical interpretation). There are plenty of books out there that do a very fine job of discussing these and other related matters.[2] While it is hard to avoid these issues completely, the debates they trigger often seem disconnected from the ground-level experience of looking at a biblical passage, reading it, being confused or inspired by it. Discussions about the minutiae of texts have a place, but there is more to be gained ultimately from an approach that examines the texts as they are and invites conversations about meaning. My own encounter with the Bible has taken a number of forms in the past two decades since I began my university studies as an undergraduate, ranging from academic biblical conferences to pre-school assemblies and other areas of my pastoral ministry, and I have become increasingly frustrated by the inaccessibility of a considerable portion of biblical scholarship to the reality of the places in which the Bible is being read (and misread). The problem of the Western obsession with sin, so often the starting point for interpretation, is that it is invariably fixed, lacking in compassion, and dominated by racial, sexual, gender and tribal interests.[3] Too often we hear that such-and-such an opinion is not 'biblical', implying the Bible speaks with a unified voice on any matter, and saying far more about the desire of some to have power and control. Perhaps ironically, any claim to 'orthodoxy' needs to be generous, not exclusive; voices 'at the margin' have as much right to be heard as those 'at the centre'.[4]

What this book does aim to do is to encourage the asking of questions, knowing that it is not possible to obtain all the answers, allowing for an encounter with God in the spaces in between. This is itself a path of exploration that is rooted in our own particularity as children of God, allowing our own weakness to be held by God's generous grace. It is an approach modelled by the Wisdom tradition of the Old Testament, present in the New Testament, and which involves the continuing search for meaning in life.[5] This search involves living and learning together despite our differences. As has so often been demonstrated, however, it is the negotiating of those differences that so often makes the Bible seem remote and flat, when what we have in the Bible is a vibrant and varied collection of books that leave plenty of room for disagreement and debate.[6] To encounter the Bible is to stand on holy ground, and any debate about it has something to do with God whether we acknowledge that or not.[7]

The art critic Barnett Newton once said that sculpture is often something we bump into when trying to get a better look at a painting.[8] The Bible is itself something we often 'bump' into when trying to get a perspective on our lives or on someone else's life. Transitional events such as baptisms, weddings and funerals typically contain readings from the Bible. If you are a regular churchgoer, the lectionary provides texts that we might not otherwise choose to encounter.[9] Most people are still familiar with the Lord's Prayer, Psalm 23 and Paul's 'hymn to love' in 1 Corinthians 13. Then, of course, we encounter the Bible at key points in the Christian year such as Christmas and Easter. Much like a sculpture, the Bible needs to be properly appreciated through direct encounter: an object in several dimensions. It is not monolithic, but is a library of books ranging across times and cultures. The English title 'Bible' comes from the Greek word *biblia*, which is plural, meaning 'books'. Certainly the Bible contains a collection that is stable, what we call a 'canon', an accepted grouping and order of books providing a 'rule' or authority that holds the texts together.[10] An analogy from the world of art helps here when thinking about the way in which the Bible holds together multiple texts. A description of

> **Risk is an inherent part of the story that unfolds in the Bible**

an exhibition that brings together works of art from many different time periods, called simply 'Brought Together', reads:

> collections of art lead something of a double life. Physically, they are mainly orderly and stable things – carefully catalogued and preserved for as long as possible in carefully controlled environments. But their meanings are nowhere near as stable. They change minute by minute, in response to the thoughts and enthusiasms of present-day viewers and the works of other artists.[11]

Paintings are kept safe in galleries, but perhaps there is a risk of overprotecting the Bible in carefully controlled environments such as the church, and the lecture room? Risk, however, is often a necessary part of life, and risk is an inherent part of the story that unfolds in the Bible.[12]

It takes time

This book also suggests that making sense of the Bible is a process that takes time. The need to read and engage slowly runs against the grain of Western culture, where speed typically means success and intelligence.[13] There is a serious problem with attempts to make the Bible readable in 10 words, or 100 minutes, because that hardly makes the Bible more attractive, nor does it allow the richness or diversity of texts to be fully appreciated. I vividly remember receiving, when I was ordained in 2005, what my fellow ordinands and I nicknamed the 'credit-crunch' Bible, which consists of the New Testament, Psalms and Proverbs. 'What about the rest of it?' I wanted to ask the bishop. It is rather like looking at a painting reproduced on a T-shirt or a mug. Gone are the intricate details of the brushwork and the vibrancy of the colours. 'Never trust a placemat,' writes the art critic Justin Paton.[14] Such a reductionist approach to the Bible typically elevates the 'good bits' over the 'bad' or 'boring' bits. Walter Brueggemann says that 'the text lingers'.[15] Of course, it is not just the text itself that 'lingers' but the trajectory of events contained therein that can linger too. In the incident of the woman caught in adultery recorded in John 7, Jesus writes on the ground. What was he writing? Much ink has been spilled on this mystery. Perhaps, however, the answer lies not in *what* he wrote, but in the act of writing itself. Archbishop Rowan Williams suggests that Jesus 'hesitates':

> He does not draw a line, fix an interpretation, tell the woman who she is and what her fate should be. He allows a moment, a longish moment, in which people are given time to see themselves differently precisely because he refuses to make the sense they want.[16]

Unfortunately, we live in a world of full-blown and instant opinion, and the notion that meaning requires finality, when it does not. Stories don't so much give closure as allow for moments of *dis*closure.[17] The reader needs to be prepared to wrestle critically and creatively with the parts of the Bible that seem to be the most confusing, fantastical and abhorrent. It is ultimately about finding an appropriate balance. Rather like a child looking at a painting of soap bubbles and making her cheeks go 'pop', the painting holds us in a moment, but the child's sense of the inevitable moves that moment on.[18] The texts linger, but they don't stay static. If we don't strive for that balance, that patience, then we surely court unimaginative interpretation that defies our heritage. The 'hermeneutical space' that we all inhabit is broad, yet in the present climate of debates about aspects of Christian belief it is being narrowed by an unwillingness to engage in critical and creative conversation, both with the text and with each other. We can only really engage in conversation if we feel able to, or invited to, and too often conversations seem to exclude rather than invite participation by everyone.[19]

Hospitality

One of the predominant motifs in the Bible that has produced many book-length studies is that of hospitality: of God's generous hospitality, and of our own hospitality to others through following the example of Christ.[20] The point here is that you can't experience hospitality unless you are willing to become vulnerable, to engage, to listen, learn and, crucially, contribute to the process of dialogue with the text, and with others. In order to be truly attentive to someone or some*thing* requires energy; it is not about passively letting it 'wash over us'. To be truly present to each other is to face Christ in each other, and if we face Christ in each other, then lives can be transformed. Too often the level of humility and vulnerability that is required to interpret the Bible is flattened by arrogance and a desire for power and sadly, the Church is often the worst offender. No wonder then that the vast majority of people who might 'bump' into the Bible are either indifferent to it, or crushed and confused by it.

> Too often the level of humility and vulnerability that is required to interpret the Bible is flattened by arrogance

The chapters of this book represent stages in the (patient) process of the search for meaning. The Polynesian artist Fatu Feu'u suggests that we need to 'go back to origins to find solutions'. Chapter 1, which is perhaps the most in-depth of the chapters, concentrates on the theme of stories contained in the Bible, and related to this, how we tell those stories so as to allow our own lives to draw meaning from the texts, and to contribute meaning to them. This latter exercise is very much the aim of Alan Jacobs, whose work on the role of testimony and the Christian life has influenced my own thinking in this area.[21] Significantly, this desire to go back to origins, to retell, and in so doing to reinterpret for a 'present' context, is a process that is found constantly in the Bible. The author of John's Gospel (re-)presents the 'nativity' of Jesus in a way that is deliberately evocative of the creation story in Genesis 1. In Acts 17 when Paul stands to speak before the assembled crowd in the Athenian Areopagus, his testimony starts with 'the beginning' ('God who made the world and everything in it', 17.24). Even the book of Revelation, perhaps the most misunderstood book in the Bible, begins to make some sense when we read it against the creative struggle first presented in the book of Genesis, the Bible's first book.

While we acknowledge the diversity of stories within the Bible, we must not ignore the observation that for most, the Bible is encountered as a single collection (a literal, physical 'book') and that this 'book' has what a television producer friend of mine once described as 'a narrative arc'. Yet if we take this particular 'arc' to be the covenantal 'arc' (or 'bow') of the flood narrative in Genesis 9.13, then it is fair to say that the stories that make up the colours and contours of that arc represent the variety of paths that prevail. The covenant has its root in the relationship between God and his 'chosen people' Israel, and yet God's 'chosen people' are not God's 'frozen people' (they have a mind and move about), and the narrative 'arc' does not present itself in an orderly manner.[22] The 'narrative arc' isn't quite how we might imagine it to be. It is anything but 'neat and tidy'.[23]

Chapter 2 explores the theme of 'contexts'. I owe an appreciation of the importance of context in how we find meaning in the Bible to my undergraduate studies and in particular to the work of Professor Philip Esler and the community of biblical scholars known as 'The Context Group', who gather annually to discuss their own research, but do so very firmly rooted in their Christian faith with a strong desire to bridge the gap between their scholarship and Christian life. 'Context' can mean a variety of things, of course, and in this chapter we explore different types of contexts: the literal context in which the texts were written, and the contexts that we the readers try to faithfully inhabit when we encounter those texts. For this latter area I owe a great debt to another of my former teachers, A. K. M. Adam, who helped balance my 'youthful' enthusiasm for the context of the text with a more stringent and self-conscious examination of what it actually 'means' to read the text.[24]

Chapter 3 bears the title 'Encounters'. Here we briefly explore both the heritage of our interpretative tradition and the variety of approaches that have been offered to help us find meaning, all the while wrestling with the reality that just because we have plenty of choice it does not follow that we are more 'free' (as any trip to the cereal aisle of a supermarket will tell you). Insights from other creative media (particularly the world of art) remind us, too, that often the way we 'encounter' (and perhaps 'bump' into) is through direct experience where the texts are being proclaimed, pictured or performed.[25] The encounter should leave us wanting to discern more about the life of the text. In that way, 'hear what the Spirit is saying to the Church' might be a more helpful liturgical invitation to respond to a reading than the declaration 'this is the word of the Lord'.[26]

Chapter 4 begins to set the tone for how we might continue our task of making sense of the Bible: through examining the medium of 'conversations'. The way to make anyone listen is not to shout, but rather to speak quietly and clearly (perhaps even to whisper). In 1 Kings 19 Elijah encounters God in the 'still small voice' rather than the louder options that were available to him. There are countless examples of conversations in the texts of the Bible, and of the search for meaning in those conversations: Job's dialogue with his friends about his life situation, Jesus' conversation with the woman at the well in John 4 in which he reveals his true identity for the first time ('I am [he]', 4.26), to name just two. The purpose of conversation is ultimately that some sort of connection is made. Connection is not about thinking exactly the same thing, but it does not negate 'the complex unity of God's purpose'.[27] As this excerpt from E. M. Forster's novel *Howards End* suggests, connection is made to achieve an important outcome:

> *Only connect!* That was the whole of her sermon. Only connect the prose and the passion and both will be exalted, and human love will be seen at its height. Live in fragments no longer.

We should not just be connecting with the elements we can see or know for ourselves; we should be seeking out the voices in the conversation that are missing (not just the voices of present-day readers, but the voices contained in the texts themselves). Furthermore, the issue of language itself becomes relevant. We encounter the texts of the Bible in translation, and translation is itself an act of interpretation. Then, of course, there are those elements in conversation that are unspoken, and perhaps even more open to misinterpretation. Yet followed faithfully and actively, the hermeneutical process can lead to greater meaning through an appreciation of the disparate voices that are participants in the conversation between ourselves and the texts, and between ourselves and those with whom we are in dialogue. This is very much at the heart of traditions that form part of our Christian heritage, particularly the Jewish rabbinical method of interpretation. Ultimately there is truly something of value at stake in the conversation, particularly if we acknowledge the desire to know more about ourselves and about God when we encounter the texts. Hermeneutical theories are all very well, but the 'So what?' question lingers as we seek further meaning in more overtly theological questions, such as 'What is God like?' The conversation doesn't end with the interpretation; it continues, held by God's overwhelming grace.

When all is said and done, this book is about more than making sense of the Bible; it is about making sense of who we are in relationship to God. The incarnation is surely one of the most profoundly engaging and risk-taking images that the Bible offers us. The occasion of God fully embracing humanity in all its messy diversity is an active and dynamic reality that rightly requires the perspective of a variety of angles. It is no wonder that the story of the incarnation is presented in different ways by the Gospel writers (Matthew 1.18—2.23; Luke 2.1–20; John 1.1–18), and the meaning of it is teased out by numerous other references in the New Testament, most notably in the Pauline letters (Philippians 2.6–11, to cite one example). It is here that we perhaps need to return to the 'What?' questions, scrutinizing what it is we are looking at, and from which perspective. The diversity of stories makes us want to know more deeply what it all means.[28] At the same time, if we are willing to acknowledge that diversity is inherent to the very texts we are seeking to make meaning of, then that search for meaning allows many voices to be heard.

An art installation entitled *Something Transparent (please go round the back)* featured the raftered ceiling of a portion of an art gallery reproduced on the gallery floor, contained in an area bounded by walls with two viewing areas. Except it wasn't at all obvious to me what I was meant to be looking at, even when I walked round the other side (as instructed by the title of the piece). It was only when I asked a member of the gallery staff for an explanation that it became clear – well, sort of – but then that was the point.[29] It all depends on your frame of reference, and where you are standing (literally). Through the asking of questions, the pondering of meaning, this book suggests that there is more than one lesson to be learned, and that in the words of the art critic and writer Justin Paton, it may well be that 'you find the map you need only after the trip has ended'.[30]

1

Stories

—•—•—•—

'It's all about the story'

(advertisement on the side of a bus for
a television company)

On Saturday 20 February 2010, the public reading of the whole
Bible in Durham Cathedral came to an end. Pat Francis, the
co-ordinator of the 'Big Read', said:

> On this final day of the Read we heard read these words from
> 1 Timothy 4.13 – *'pay attention to the public reading of Scripture.'*
> This has been fulfilled by 506 readers from an ecumenical list
> of denominations . . . and represents 106 individual readers, 30
> teams, and 7 schools. 928 people spent time listening during the
> Read, and the children from the 7 schools, along with all who
> shared in this event, will have brought back to family, friends,
> neighbours and work colleagues their scripts and the news of
> what they had read, of what they had heard. The proclaiming
> of Scripture grows beyond the Cathedral.[1]

Stories, or more particularly the proclamation of stories, are a
vital part of many cultures in our world, but perhaps less so in
many Western contexts. Stories can have immense power, and
the ability for our imagination to be captured by 'a good yarn'
is a very real one. The reappearance of the *Doctor Who* franchise
on UK television (and exported to other countries) brought
back the adventures of this most famous of time travellers
to the highly valued prime-time Saturday evening family

viewing slot. The season finale of series three, 'The Last of the Time Lords', depicted the Doctor's assistant, Martha Jones, travelling across Earth for a year. For most of the episode we were led to believe that she was collecting parts for a particular weapon that would destroy the arch-enemy known as The Master. As the episode reached a critical point, Martha Jones revealed that she was not travelling on Earth to locate parts for a gun, but instead to tell people stories about the Doctor so that at a particular moment everyone would think about the Doctor, and the collective energy of their thoughts would in fact overcome The Master. It was the power of stories rather than technology that won the day. When this episode was first broadcast, on 30 June 2007, it produced a viewing figure of 8.61 million.[2] While the *Doctor Who* franchise undoubtedly has a life of its own, a large part of the story of its success lies in the skill of the writers who put the story together.

Aside from the world of film and television, the telling of stories can play an important role in shaping and affirming national identity. Following any major event or disaster, it is commonplace for people to want to share the story of where they were and what they were doing when they heard the news. The telling of stories can also have a redemptive quality, as the process in South Africa following the end of apartheid, known as the Truth and Reconciliation Commission, has demonstrated, along with other similar processes of restorative justice.

When it comes to the Bible, encountering its variety of stories is rather like making your way through an art gallery. Which route do you take? An orderly one (as suggested by the official guide book), or do you go with your own sense of direction, heading straight for the *Mona Lisa* bypassing countless other paintings? The point of encounter, of looking at stories, is the point at which we start, before the process of interpretation begins (although it is sometimes hard to separate the two). In his article 'The Literal Sense of Scripture', Rowan Williams advocates an approach to reading the stories of the Bible in a 'literal sense'. By 'literal' he means reading with attention and patience, story by story, allowing for plurality of genres, for occasions of conflict where texts appear to work against each other, and moments when the text just doesn't seem to make sense. The word 'literal' does not equate in meaning with more fundamentalist readings which ultimately shrink the meaning of the texts.[3] Much like the 'Big Read' mentioned above, perhaps we need to spend more time simply *reading* the texts as stories, rather than taking elements from different stories in order to work out where an overall sense of 'unity' lies. This latter approach is more naturally predisposed to be agenda-driven (whether consciously or not), stemming from a desire to uphold one version of events over all others.[4] This attention to 'taking time' in story-by-story reading is unsettling to a Western culture dominated by speed.[5]

Individual story-units in the Bible are sometimes called 'pericopes', a word that is not understood by modern word-processing programs, with spell-checkers set to change 'pericope' to 'periscope'. Yet there may well be meaning to this, for when read carefully stories alert us to deeper 'movements or rhythms' within a text, meanings that are located above and beyond where the boundaries of the text appear to lie.[6] Sometimes we need to look up and around in order to comprehend what it is we are looking at (as my encounter with the art installation referred to in the Introduction taught me).[7] A story-driven reading isn't as naive as it might sound, and it certainly allows for a more

> A story-driven reading gives permission for a great variety of readings . . . to be in conversation with one another

honest approach that invites contributions from all sides of the interpretative spectrum.[8] Moreover, it permits the boundaries of meaning to change depending on whether we read a story on its own, or within a particular book, or indeed within a particular section of the Bible. It does not advocate the elevation of one interpretation over another, but rather gives permission for a great variety of readings – of even just one story (pericope) – to be in conversation with one another. In this way, reading the Bible creates a proper sense of unity that does not come from everyone thinking the same thing,

> but from the obligation to bear with one another, to testify to the truth as we have received it, and to continue to show forbearance and patience in the shared hope that when all things are revealed, the Revealer will also display the manner in which our diverse interpretations form a comprehensive concord in ways that now elude our comprehension.[9]

But what is it exactly that we are reading? A colleague of mine once began a session on how Anglicans read the Bible by asking the assembled group what title they might give to the Bible. At first, the reaction was, 'It's already got a title: *The Bible*,' but following an initial sense of puzzlement, the group pondered this question and offered a variety of suggestions:

The Word is out
God's story
The meaning of everything
42 (from Douglas Adams' *The Hitchhiker's Guide to the Galaxy*, the number that apparently answers everything that can be asked in life about life)
God, Jesus and the Holy Spirit
The story of salvation
People get it wrong, God puts it right
The Good Book

15

It was, as it turned out, a considerably more difficult exercise than it first appeared. It brought about a realization that 'the Bible' is indeed a whole series of stories. Brought together as 'canon' they stand alone, each constituent part offering an angle on what might best be described as a 'God-shaped' story. But the question remains, 'What is it that we are reading?' The saying goes that every picture tells a story, but pictures are not always titled. To make matters more confusing, sometimes the title a painting is given is simply *Untitled*. Placed next to such a painting by the artist Richard Serra the helpful comment to the pondering viewer reads:

> Perhaps art is a visual experience. Rather than offering external explanations, they [the artist] want us to engage with what is physically there – the contrasts of dark and light, relations between shapes and the impressions of harmony or tensions that result ... visual art is special because it says something that is difficult to capture in words, and that includes words on a wall label.[10]

This provides a helpful insight into what a 'literal' approach to reading the Bible might involve. An analogous model was in fact proposed by Brooke Foss Westcott in the late nineteenth century. Westcott held that the details of the biblical narratives mattered intensely. Although it was important to view the texts as a whole, from a distance, there was ultimately more to be gained from paying close attention to detail. To put it succinctly:

> Interpretation for the believer is thus a shuttling between the closest possible reading of the text, with all the resources available, and the repeated attempt to find words to articulate the complex unity that is being uncovered.[11]

I once led a Bible study with a group of women on the Magnificat, which is found in the first chapter of Luke's Gospel. Surprisingly, it was the verse immediately after the words of the Magnificat that attracted the most discussion. In 1.56 we read: 'And Mary remained with her about three months and then returned to her home.' A brief glance at academic commentaries on Luke's Gospel reveals that this sentence does not attract much comment, if any, yet it was this verse that invited further exploration precisely because it involved imaginative reflection upon events 'off the page'. We will look more at the importance of imaginative reflection later on in this book, but it makes the important point here that time spent with stories can often enable specific details to be noticed that we might otherwise pass over.

Genre

The Bible, as we have already asserted, is a collection of books, within which we find collections of stories. The use of the word 'book', however, needs some qualification at this point, since at the time of composition there were only scrolls, and copies of scrolls. Moreover, each 'book' was likely produced by multiple authors, often in different locations, over different periods of time and crucially, writing in the languages of Hebrew, Aramaic and Greek, using different genres.[12] The book of Revelation, for example, can only be fully understood if we take into account its apocalyptic genre. This helps us understand the fantastical imagery in this book, which makes little sense to us, but makes every sense with regard to the genre that provides the framework through which we encounter this text. Attention to the variety of genres is also helpful because not every pericope in the Bible may neatly be defined as a 'story', at least in our own understandings of what stories are; it depends on the genre of what we are reading. So we use 'story' lightly in the sense that each narrative unit is ultimately telling us something about the story of God (this is how we choose to view it from the perspective of faith). This is useful to bear in mind when we encounter what to all intents and purposes *looks* like a book (pages of writing between two covers). At the same time, although we encounter the Bible first and foremost as a work of literature, the stories themselves emerged from oral tradition and were rooted in a belief in God who created the world, sustained it and redeemed it through Jesus Christ. So we are dealing with multiple layers: the Bible is a pluralistic text, and the translations that we have are themselves interpretations. This should give us some encouragement when we try to make sense of the Bible as a whole; it reminds us of the need for patience when it comes to this process of searching for meaning, and awareness that language is often a barrier to that meaning.

Why those stories?

What are the stories that are contained in the Bible, and why *those* stories and not others? Both these questions can, on one level, be answered quite simply: the 'what' and 'why' are because of a relationship, or rather, many relationships. There is not a single story in the Bible that does not have its origin in a relationship: with God, with other people, or with communities. Paul's letter to Philemon is a good example of this. Being such a short letter, it is easy to understand why it might not have made it into the New Testament canon. But the importance and authority of its author Paul secured its place. The relationship that Paul had with his communities made them value his writings highly. Part of the dynamics of that relationship, as the stories themselves reveal, are the many ways in which people *respond*. Of course, when it comes to the letters of the New Testament, we don't have direct access to the response of the communities to which the letters were sent, and this is

why the 'stories' of Paul's letters need to be interpreted dramatic-
ally, taking into account their genre as letters.[13] One almost
has to imagine a conversation happening; these are not 'flat'
documents. This sense of conversation (direct and indirect) is
the meaning and importance of the covenantal theme that
is sustained throughout the Bible, and is more of an active
state of being rather than a story told and that alone. The
covenantal theme works beyond the boundaries of the texts, as
the stories are received, valued and discerned in communities,
in multiple contexts and places. In this way, the insight of
N. T. Wright may be helpful here: that the Bible is like a five-act
Shakespearean play. The fifth act remains unwritten and it is
up to 'us' to improvise its contents while remaining 'in character'.[14]
Yet even with this a note of caution should be registered over
who determines the meaning of 'character' and whether more
than one expression of how that character behaves is permitted
to join the conversation. The challenge inherent in this is
hardly new. The twentieth-century French philosopher Michel
de Certeau discussed at some length the challenge for Christianity to remain faithful to the inaugural event (the God-shaped
story contained in the Bible), and yet the necessity to assert
difference from those beginnings.[15]

Space here does not allow for a detailed examination of
all of the stories in the Bible.[16] The present aim is to engage
with aspects of *how* the Bible tells its stories rather than simply
to analyse their narrative content (which is what a more traditional commentary does in the process known as 'exegesis').[17]
This might be more boldly asserted as identification of the
potential *effects* that the stories have, and although I acknowledge that this may be a risky endeavour, it does reinforce
the point about relationships made earlier, that the fullest of
meaning comes from appreciation of the relationships within
the texts and the relationship that the readers have both with

God and with the texts. Any identification of story-types that I may choose is, of course, generated by me, and others may disagree with the category descriptions that follow. But the point is to try at least to be realistic with that 'literal' sense of what it might mean for individuals and communities to read the text 'as it is'.

I suggested above that interpretation follows a reading of text (in the way that, liturgically speaking, a sermon follows the readings), yet the distance between the acts of reading and interpretation is sometimes very small indeed. It is actually hard for our imagination not to engage straight away with what we are reading or hearing. One of my regular commitments is taking assemblies in our local primary school. Telling stories to the children often produces instant reactions because imaginations are engaged by what they hear and, crucially, by what they *see*. I recall telling the story of John the Baptist heralding the gospel message as reported in the first chapter of Mark's Gospel. To 'inhabit' the persona of John I put on a rather dubious-looking brown coat, tied a leather belt around my waist, and wore a fake beard and wig. I held aloft a jar of honey, and because (not surprisingly) I could not locate any locusts I found a large rubber spider and waved that in the air. I had not anticipated that the very youngest children were rather perturbed by the spider, and so a message of reassurance in the midst of John's strident proclamation had to be improvised! Children, by and large, are not inhibited from employing their imaginative gifts in response to a story in the way adults often are, and I still get comments about my telling of the 'John' story to this day. Walter Brueggemann comments, 'the need for imagination may also suggest that the handling of the text as an insider requires of us

> I found a large rubber spider and waved that in the air

energy and boldness if its new pertinence is to be perceived and received among us'.[18]

All this points to the need to take seriously the performative nature of the stories. The advert mentioned at the beginning of this chapter depicted a man and a woman crouching near to the ground. The perspective of the picture was 'from the ground up', almost on a level with the two figures. The scene appeared to be rural, and it looked as though the woman was interviewing the man, who was perhaps a farmer talking about an issue related to his land. By asserting, 'it's all about the story', the viewer is encouraged to delve deeper into what might lie behind the available (visual and performative) information. But the point here is to unfold the broad canvas of the story that lies open before us and invites us to react, perhaps even *demands* that we react in some way. Our canvas isn't necessarily flat (to return to the covenantal arc image that is by no means neat and tidy); it may well fall and fold, depending on our perspective. The artist Philippa Blair's paintings defy being hung neatly like more conventional artworks; on one occasion when she was painting, her canvas dropped inadvertently, which caused her to move away from traditional formats to focus on constructed surfaces. Thus the canvas of her art droops in different ways wherever it is hung on the wall, and no two displays of her work will ever look the same. In order to view her work, therefore, one has to study the textures and contours and observe the ways in which the colours reflect off one another in that particular context: the art is not flat, nor is our viewing of it!

Types of story

If we consider for a moment how the Bible presents us with stories, two points emerge: first, the need to get a sense of the variety of story-types (what they are in a 'literal' sense); and second, the pulling together of all these types into a proposed narrative model, which I want to suggest is something along the lines of developing an actual 'theology of reading'. What I offer here, therefore, is a suggestion of some 'types' of story along with accompanying textual references for the reader to examine. This is followed by illustration of a narrative model from Walter Brueggemann's work on making sense of the Bible. None of this is exhaustive (I would not wish to claim that), but it might help our search for meaning. Indeed, time spent with any one of these stories, simply reading them as they are, may ultimately allow for some of the deeper rhythms of meaning to emerge.

Rowan Williams writes that 'the setting out of an historical story becomes indispensable to the human quest for truth ... the gospel isolates events rather like looking through the wrong end of a telescope to give distance and perspective to otherwise confused details'.[19] These words helpfully shed light upon our reflecting on *how* the Bible tells its stories; not only that, but how it is possible for us to read them so that our own sense of (literal) distance is given the perspective that allows for meaning and sense to take shape. The process of presenting varieties of stories and the ways in which those stories can be held together and connected in different ways finds an analogy in the world of art. The New Zealand artist Richard Killeen is well known for his cut-outs in which he selects and manipulates images of his place and time. Every installation of his art is unique, resulting from 'an open pictoral system, its elements variously drawn from their storage box like so many specimens of their kind. Including everything from the quotidian to the arcane, Killeen's endlessly re-arrangeable pictograms capture our stories as they tell his.'[20]

A major exhibition of Killeen's paintings was held in Auckland in 1999. The title of the exhibition, 'Stories We Tell Ourselves', was taken from two of Killeen's largest works: *Stories we tell ourselves* and *Stories we tell each other*. Although Killeen's artworks themselves constitute diverse and potentially endless meanings, they can gain deeper meaning through their collective identities as 'stories of place', 'stories of gender', 'stories of war', 'stories of his own art' and 'stories of the self'. Identification of individual story-types is one stage in the process, but a related stage is how those stories may be held together to provide meaning.[21]

Before we explore in some more detail the 'theology of reading' that the above comments point to, we need briefly to examine the variety of story-types that often confuse meaning rather than clarify it. Throughout the Bible (and in no particular order), there are books and stories within those books that dislocate (Exodus and the narrative of the exile); stories that contain secrets (the so-called 'Messianic Secret' in Mark's Gospel); stories that contradict (Ezra-Nehemiah's prohibition against foreign wives and the book of Ruth's blatant contradiction of this); stories that are instructive (Exodus 25—28 with its details of how to construct the Ark of the Covenant, the Tabernacle and the sacred vestments); stories that exclude (Leviticus and the apparent strictness of the legislation within that); stories that challenge (Revelation); stories that comfort (Psalms); stories that are prescriptive (Exodus and the giving of the Mosaic Law); stories that redeem and address the statement, 'This is not the way it is supposed to be, God' (Job); stories that uplift and motivate (Acts); stories that repel (Jephthah's daughter in Judges 11); stories that are extraordinary (the accounts of Jesus' miracles contained in the Gospels); stories of wonder and joy (the birth of Jesus as narrated in Matthew and Luke); stories of lament (Lamentations); stories that impart wisdom (Proverbs); stories that don't look like stories (many of the letters in the New Testament); and stories that deal with one subject from different perspectives (the life, death and resurrection of Jesus as told in the four Gospels of the New Testament).

This list, while not by any means 'complete', is helped by
Walter Brueggemann's own narrative model, by which he
divides stories into groups: the 'primal narrative' (the basics
of the story, the most important details, such as the liturgical
confession contained in Deuteronomy 26.5–9), or even the
'kerygmatic' passages (those elements of teaching that are
foundational to the articulation of faith) in the New Testament
(such as at 1 Corinthians 3.1); the 'expanded narrative' (what
Brueggemann defines as 'a collection of all the ways in which
the primal narrative has been perceived and handled', thus
Genesis 12—50 expands the promise made to 'my father who
was a wandering Aramean'); 'derivative narratives' (the 'what
happens next' part of the story, such as the Acts of the Apostles);
the 'literature of institutionalization' (the law-defining book
of Leviticus); the 'literature of mature theological reflection'
(such as Romans); and the 'literature of instruction and voca-
tion' (much of the Prophets, and the letters of Paul).[22] The
advantage of this narrative model is that it allows the stories
of the Bible to 'stand on their own', but makes sense of some
of the deeper ways in which they permit meaning to emerge.
It also provides an answer to the desire for the Bible to mean
something other than be just a fragmented collection of
stories.

Meaning interrupted

A considerable portion of our own interaction with stories
comes through hearing them being proclaimed. In part a con-
tinuation of the oral tradition that lies behind the stories in the
Bible, the proclamation of texts, in a modern sense, brings the
stories into the public sphere, certainly in the church, but often
the 'market place' too. It is in the latter of these arenas that a
meaning can be obscured precisely because of an unwillingness

to engage with the story for what it is in the truly 'literal' sense.[23] A prime example of meaning interrupted is the Christmas story. One year, my local city council decided to hold a 'Winter Light Festival' rather than celebrate Christmas. The result was a blend of brass band-accompanied traditional Christmas carols, illuminated symbols of sun, moon and stars, inflatable Santa Claus balloons, and all a short distance from the very spot where Cranmer, Latimer and Ridley were burned at the stake for their Christian faith. Rather like a recent survey that suggested that many children believe that the film character Buzz Lightyear was the first man on the moon, the Winter Light Festival created uncertainty and confusion, and interrupted the meaning of what the event was trying to mask: the incarnation.[24] Alongside the performative nature by which we can encounter stories, they are often *in themselves* proclamation or argument. To return to the Apostle Paul, I once heard it said that reading any of Paul's letters is like watching someone thinking! The New Zealand artist Colin McCahon, whose paintings are often inspired by his Christian faith, began his career as a theatre-set designer and thought of his paintings as

> The story itself is 'riveting' . . . Jesus did not tell it as an 'academic lecture'

spaces that you could 'vicariously clamber through'.[25] Writing about the parable of the crafty steward in Luke 16.1–8, David Kahan reflects that because the story itself is 'riveting' it is likely that Jesus did not tell it as an 'academic lecture':

> more plausible is that Jesus created a playing space, a stage as it were, between himself and his followers where the action was to take place . . . For two millennia Scripture has been transmitted as verbal performed art; so it should not be surprising that one characteristic biblical organizing principle, the chiasm (the crossing of two opposing thoughts in the form of an X), closely resembles the acts, movements and interaction found in theater.[26]

The suggestion that stories are products of eyewitness testimony is of particular interest, since it brings to the fore questions of history and memory, and asks us to consider that the New Testament Gospels in particular are the products of authors who are deeply engaged theologians and not just mouthpieces. This also helps us understand why it is that we have not one but four Gospels, each with a particular slant on the story of Jesus. In his book *Jesus and the Eyewitnesses*, Richard Bauckham brings together theological and historical arguments. The historical argument is that the eyewitnesses to the events described in the Gospels remained the sources of the narratives, and that the Gospels themselves are more reflective of the ways in which eyewitnesses told their stories.[27] The theological argument is that the category of testimony provides a more helpful way of approaching understandings of Jesus than the 'Jesus of history' versus the 'Christ of faith' debate that has been so dominant in scholarship. It suggests that faith and fact are both integral and vital to the way in which the narratives are retold, and that this in fact frees up the narratives from constant historical scrutiny, because they were never intended to be history, at least not in our modern understanding of what 'history' is.

Stories are not isolated from the context in which they are told, and this is where interpretation can help us to appreciate the time and distance between us and the story that we are encountering. Stories 'mark time', both the time in which they were told and eventually written down (which may be different), and our own time. Anyone who has ever preached should have an awareness of this, for part of the task of sermon-writing is to proclaim the integrity of the text being preached on, and what relevance it might have afresh in a contemporary and often localized setting.[28]

The Australian author John Marsden's *Tomorrow* series tells the story of how a group of teenagers respond to the surprise invasion of their country. Told from the perspective of one of the characters in the story, Ellie, the narrative is written in the narrator's present.[29] Near the end of the first book, *Tomorrow, When the War Began*, Ellie reflects: 'It's hard to work out where stories begin – I seem to remember saying that at the start of this one. And it's hard to work out where they end, too. Our story hasn't ended yet . . .' Events unfold as if time had passed, but as if they have not yet happened, which is rather mind-bending, but it works very effectively; in fact, when we recount events in our lives we often do the same quite naturally. Ellie herself comments in the last book, *The Other Side of Dawn*:

> When I had set out to write what we'd done in the war, it was like a public thing. We wanted to know that we'd made a difference on a big scale. I wrote it because we wanted to be remembered, because we wanted to believe our lives had some meaning. We wanted to know we hadn't passed through the world unchanged, and that we hadn't left the world unchanged. We didn't want to come and go from the planet without leaving a mark.

The story is told because of the relationship that the narrator has with her own story and that of her companions and a desire to impart wisdom to others for the ongoing journeys of their lives through the shared knowledge of what has taken place. In this way the narrative is future-oriented, which is, of course, reflected in the title *Tomorrow*. Walter Brueggemann comments with regard to the stories of the Bible that they 'are not past-oriented but are set toward the future'.[30]

Analysis of the Greek of Mark's Gospel provides an excellent example of the thoughtful and intricate use of tenses in the proclamation of the story of Jesus. Mark frequently uses the present tense, a feature often ignored in translations, with the exception of that by Nicholas King, which renders the present in a literal way. The result is that although Mark is recounting events that have already happened, when we read the story it is as though we are participants in it in a present sense, and in a way that is meant to encourage even us in our contemporary setting in the continuing and future tasks of discipleship.[31] Another way of looking at this important issue of tense is through the lens of an interpretative approach

> We are participants in the story ... in a way that is meant to encourage ... us ... in the continuing and future tasks of discipleship

known as 'bystander theology', which refers both to bystanders within the story and to ourselves as onlookers. David Kahan writes:

> as an alternative to arriving on the scene *after* something has happened, the theologian arrives on the scene *before* the action has taken place. In approaching the biblical texts from the opposite end as if he or she were an onlooker attempting to discover what is happening, a particular biblical moment is reconstructed. The text is read with a forward movement, as if one had been there at the beginning as an observer with an advantageous viewpoint ... faced with a biblical text that is in many ways a flat, unarticulated surface, the exegete turns to the principles of fine arts, to painting, architecture, sculpture, and certainly to performances found in theater.[32]

This also has considerable interpretative value, as we may ask to what extent it is possible to return to a story and re-present it with new meaning without negating prior meaning or denying openness to yet more meanings in the future, or that other contexts may demand. The Bible *makes* sense by inviting us to make

> The Bible *makes* sense by inviting us to make sense of our own lives

sense of our own lives, and the lives of the communities of which we are part, alongside the stories that we encounter.[33] This is not to say that the stories in the Bible constitute a 'self-help' manual, though this might effectively be the case for some people, but the stories do considerably more than just that because they are ultimately incorporating our lives into the God-shaped story that itself shapes who we are. To put it another way, the stories themselves both constitute and create identity. This is by no means a recent revelation. In the New Testament the letters of Paul represent the working out of the parameters of a newly forming faith which (for Paul) is rooted very firmly in the already established narrative of God's dealings with Israel. Paul has to reinterpret his whole life story in the light of his encounter with the risen Christ on the road to Damascus (as told in Acts 9.1–19; 22.6–16; 26.12–18).

One of the consequences of recognizing a relationship between deeper meanings that may reside within the texts, the need to persevere with those texts, and the ways in which we may be able to tell our stories as part of the larger story, may most helpfully be described as a 'theology of reading'. The stories we tell ourselves and the stories we tell each other can (if we allow them to) constitute a redemptive endeavour. I suspect that part of the reason why the Bible often doesn't make sense is that we

> **The stories we tell ourselves and . . . each other can . . . constitute a redemptive endeavour**

have lost our capacity as a Western culture to listen to stories, to remember them, to consider them valuable and to retell them to others in ways that might be meaningful. When we do interact with stories, they usually come to us from people we do not know personally (as in the case of the *Doctor Who* series). An over-reliance on receiving stories through the media of film and television runs the risk that we have in fact lost a capacity to tell our own stories; as James Cone observes:

When people can no longer listen to others' stories, they become enclosed within their own social context, treating their distorted visions of reality as the whole truth. And then they feel that they must destroy other stories, which bear witness that life can be lived in another way.[34]

This is where meaning becomes interrupted, like the distortion of the Christmas story we encountered earlier. Far more concerning than a lack of exposure to storytelling, however, is a lack of attention to reading, and reading that takes time.[35]

In his work on narrative theology, Alan Jacobs reflects on us becoming consciously aware of telling our own stories and of thinking about our lives narratively so as to impart wisdom:

we Christians should think of our lives as emerging, developing instances of one (or more) of the various genres of the Christian life, as stories that move along recognizable paths, paths followed by our predecessors and indeed by our contemporary companions in the faith . . . if we do this, we will be better prepared for the role of traveller [Aquinas' concept of 'one on the way'], better protected from the twin dangers of presumption and despair, better able to see changes in the road as continuations of it rather than detours from it or dead ends.[36]

We will explore more of this in Chapter 4 on 'Conversations', but the example of the Letter to the Hebrews provides an interesting illustration at this point of stories told so as to impart wisdom for the 'present'. The genre of Hebrews is disputed; it appears to be more like a sermon than a letter, but a sermon that is sent nonetheless in letter form (as its ending suggests). Hebrews makes sense in its assertion of future hope in a faith that has already begun growing in the life of the Jewish believers in Christ. These are the believers that likely constitute the community that this text was intended for (whether in the Jewish diaspora or in the setting of Palestine itself) in the latter part of the first century. The meaning of faith is understood through a retrospective telling of the stories of the ancestors in chapter 11, which begins: 'Now faith is the assurance of things hoped for, the conviction of things not seen' (11.1).

The author proceeds with mention of the stories of Cain and Abel (Genesis 4); Enoch (Genesis 5); Noah (Genesis 6—9); Abraham and Sarah (Genesis 12—24); Isaac, Jacob, Esau and Joseph (Genesis 21—50); Moses (Exodus from chapter 2 onwards, Leviticus, Numbers, Deuteronomy); Rahab (Joshua 2); Gideon (Judges 6—8); Barak (Judges 4—5); Samson (Judges 13—14); Jephthah (Judges 11—12); David (1 and 2 Samuel, 1 Kings); Samuel (1 Samuel); and the prophets (not named but including, of course, Jeremiah, Amos, Hosea, Isaiah and others). Collectively, these are the 'great cloud of witnesses' whose stories precede that of Jesus, who for the author is 'the pioneer and perfecter of our faith' (12.1–2). The ancestors (and they are referred to as such) offer models of faith (for better or worse), and associated (often literal) journeys that often take unexpected turns, individuals who are companions on the way in the deep sense of that phrase as Jacobs understands it above. In our Western traditions, we are more used to encountering ancestors after death; here in Hebrews we are offered meaning through their accompanying us in our present tasks of discipleship. Although the Bible offers considerable vision of and hope for the future, as Dietrich Bonhoeffer commented, the gospel must 'exist for this world . . . in the biblical sense of the creation and of the incarnation, crucifixion, and resurrection of Jesus Christ'.[37]

Unity of purpose

Although this present chapter has shied away from unity in its assertion of the presence of many stories in the Bible, unity none-theless remains an important aspect of the process of making sense of the Bible, given its location in the context of communities that receive and interpret the texts. So it may be possible to speak of a 'unity of purpose' rather than limitless pluralities of meaning. The texts, even when read story by story, do reach their own conclusions. The Passion narrative, for example, ends with Jesus' death on the cross and his resurrection, but if the context of the reading of that text takes place over the course of Holy Week, or in some other communal setting, then the meaning of the text surely expands to encompass other understandings and perspectives that the text cannot possibly contain on its own.[38] The 'Big Read' in Durham Cathedral mentioned at the beginning of this chapter draws on this possibility of the process of reading, retelling and obtaining new meaning continuing in ways beyond what the boundaries of the texts could ever possibly imagine. Much like the characters in *The Lord of the Rings*:

> lost in a wilderness metaphorically as well as cartographically, indeed in a 'bewilderment'. But there is a pattern of events that is potentially available to them once they all get together and share information and that is available to the very careful reader through much of the book.[39]

If it is really the case that 'chaos is the score upon which reality is written', then the stories of the Bible progress against what often seems like a chaotic backdrop.[40] This is not problematic, however, since the overcoming of chaos remains a recurring feature in the texts of the Bible, from the waters of the creation in Genesis, all the way to the fantastical scenes of chaos in the book of Revelation. Chaos isn't negative; it is necessary to allow the vision of a different reality (that of God) to achieve the fullest possible resonance. The characters from *The Lord of*

> Chaos . . . is necessary to allow the vision of a different reality . . . to achieve the fullest possible resonance

the Rings in the reflection above bear a similarity to the disciples on the Emmaus road (Luke 24.13–35), who are in their own state of bewilderment; they encounter Jesus and yet do not recognize him until the end of the story, and then retell what happened to them to the other disciples once they return to Jerusalem. This is immediately followed in 24.36–43 by another resurrection appearance by Jesus, to the assembled disciples who, having just heard the Emmaus story, *still* fail to recognize Jesus when he appears to them. We, the reader, of course *know* that it is Jesus in both cases and in this sense it is possible to assert that the texts 'are not only what they are . . . [they] give more than they have'.[41] The 'giving' implies this word 'relationship', which we have already met (and which is inherent to Brueggemann's narrative model, since it is the community that gives the stories meaning), and the living out of that relationship itself takes place within community, context and place; it is to this that we turn in the next chapter.

2

Contexts

'The past is a foreign country: they do things differently there.'[1]

In the previous chapter we discussed how the Bible is full of stories, and how an appreciation of the 'literal' sense of the texts can accompany the telling of our own stories so that together they may gain meaning and sense. This first stage, of acknowledging the plain meaning of the text, is followed by an awareness of *place* and *context*, both of the text itself and of our own location as the reader. Why is this important? The social-scientific biblical scholar Bruce Malina comments: 'The problem with a fundamentalism that is interested only in what the Bible says – and not in what it means in terms of the social context in which it emerged – is that it implicitly denies the Incarnation.'[2]

Such 'flat' readings of the Bible produce one-sided interpretations, and ignore the rather obvious point that the stories of the Bible were themselves often dynamically proclaimed in context(s). That is a generalizing point, for sure, but it is a principle that needs to be asserted at the outset. It is impossible to understand the message of the prophets in the Old Testament without appreciating that they issued their prophecies in relation to contexts. In a similar way, in the New Testament John the Baptist appears in order to say boldly that the time for the proclamation of Christ is *now* (the narrative time and space in Mark 1.4–8, for example), the place is *here*

(Galilee) and the purpose is *this* (that lives may be transformed for the kingdom). Mark's narrative intent (so I suggest) is that although John literally appears at a point in time, the genre of Gospel enables his context to embrace all contexts, including our own.[3]

Bridging the gap

At the heart of an appreciation of context(s) should be a desire to be *considerate* readers. How do we 'bridge the gap' from the world of the texts to our own worlds and local communities? Biblical scholarship has in fact long been engaged in the development of interpretative paradigms that assist us with understanding the contexts of the texts, but it has been less sympathetic to the process of reading our own contexts alongside this. This is largely because biblical scholarship tends to focus on questions of 'history' rather than 'faith'; 'Did it happen?' rather than 'What does it mean for my belief in a God who creates, sustains and redeems?' What a text may mean to us is perceived as best located within the area of faith confession, which biblical scholarship has often had an uneasy relationship with.[4] However, a number of recent books have called for more work to be done in this area, and indeed a growing awareness of the 'global' nature of the contexts in which the Bible is encountered has led to the promotion of readings of the stories that draw meaning from the 'local' place in which the story is read (and what it *means* for us to read and re-read in our own contexts).[5] This is not to say that the text once meant something and now means something different. The point is that there can be continuity of meaning if we allow conversations to take place between ourselves and the texts that we encounter.[6] This present chapter examines some of the interpretative approaches that may help us to be considerate readers, and offers some more general reflections on the role of contexts in making sense of the Bible.

A priest colleague of mine (and an ardent *Doctor Who* fan) remarked to me that it would be wonderful if we could step inside the Tardis and journey back in time to follow Jesus and listen to his teachings first hand. It would certainly make sermon preparation easier, he suggested. However, time travel might not yield the desired results. Simon Holdaway, professor of archaeology at the University of Auckland, muses upon the potential drawbacks of time travel (and in so doing promotes the argument that archaeology is more useful):

> If you could travel back to a point in time, say 2000 years before now in far western New South Wales, Australia – where I have undertaken fieldwork – what would you see? The answer is probably nothing. The Aboriginal people who lived in western New South Wales were mobile so they visited places only intermittently. Between visits places were abandoned. One would have to time our arrival in a time machine rather precisely to meet anybody at all.[7]

Given the itinerant nature of Jesus' own ministry, the arrival of a time machine would likewise have to be timed rather carefully. Is it really the case, however, that archaeology can give us a closer understanding of context? In 2010, 100 objects were selected by the director of the British Museum Neil MacGregor, to tell the history of the world through a BBC Radio 4 series and a number of spin-offs, including more local-based programmes on radio and television. Objects selected included a statue of an Egyptian pharaoh, shadow puppets from Indonesia and the Sutton Hoo helmet. MacGregor commented that 'objects take us into the thought world of people in the past more directly and more subtly than anything else'.[8]

But do they really? When I spent three weeks digging in the dusty dirt of an archaeological site in Israel, I was happily trawling through the dust of what I had been assured was a tenth-century BCE domestic dwelling, only to uncover falafel wrappers from an altogether more recent time period. Objects 'take us into the thought world of people in the past more directly and more subtly than anything else'? I'm not so sure it's *that* simple – surely that's only part of the story of what it means to connect with our past? The falafel wrapper signified the meeting of a basic human need – hunger; more than that I wouldn't wish to speculate, nor should we!

Each one of us is rooted in the local, and in the particular. Like museums, perhaps, we are all treasure troves of stories, feelings, experiences, things that make us who we are; we all have a past, a present and a future, and all of this is ultimately rooted in that which we cannot fully comprehend. Objects are one thing, but our own potential for wonder and imagination, and for compassion and hope, is an altogether less tangible part of human nature, and it is this that allows us to engage with the God-shaped narrative that is the Bible. Neither time travel (which we cannot do), nor archaeology (which we can do) can deliver what we need in order to gain meaning. I am not suggesting that archaeology has not given us many valuable insights into how people have lived their lives; its scope is inevitably limited because it deals largely with objects rather than people.

In the previous chapter we mentioned the analogy of the art gallery as a place containing many different artworks, and the dilemma of which route to take through the gallery. In the same way as an art gallery provides a home for paintings, the Bible contains books of varying genres that themselves provide context by giving meaning to the stories within, the book of Revelation being perhaps the best example of this.[9] Sometimes those contexts can be transformed, giving different perspectives to their contents. In September 2010 and February 2011, following major earthquakes in the Canterbury region of the south island of New Zealand, the Christchurch Art Gallery became the civil defence centre. The gallery's exhibition space became the backdrop for the co-ordinated response to the earthquake. High-profile meetings of government ministers and local officials jostled for position among paintings and sculptures. In a similar way, biblical texts can take on different meanings depending upon *where* they are being read, and *who* is reading them. On this latter point, interpretation of the opening verses of Paul's letter to

> Biblical texts can take on different meanings depending upon *where* they are being read, and *who* is reading them

the Romans can be assisted by appreciating Paul's own Roman context. When Paul boldly declares the importance of the gospel of God at the beginning of this letter – 'the gospel concerning his Son, who was descended from David according to the flesh and was declared to be Son of God with power according to the spirit of holiness by resurrection from the dead, Jesus Christ our Lord' (1.3–4) – he is doing more than enthusiastically confessing his faith. He is likely being deliberately provocative in subversively echoing similar paeans of praise to the Roman emperor. Alongside this, the politically subversive nature of Paul's words takes on new meaning when interpreted by individuals living under military rule in our contemporary world, as I discovered when studying this letter with Fijian students I have taught.[10]

Scholarly developments in the latter part of the twentieth century produced a greater appreciation of the context of the first century in particular (the world of the New Testament), which inevitably had an effect on biblical scholarship in general. The fullness of meaning that came from the realization that Jesus was a *Jew*, and how Paul's Jewishness (and cultural complexity) informed his own re-presentation of the story of Israel are two examples of how developments in interpretation brought the texts into new light.[11] Moreover, when scholars began to speak about the variety within Judaism, a development assisted by the discovery of the Dead Sea Scrolls in the mid twentieth century, passages in the Bible that seemed to be contradictory made more sense.[12] Passages in Matthew's Gospel, for example, that appear to be 'pro-Jewish' and 'anti-Jewish' are in fact examples of an ongoing debate over identity and aren't really meant as 'pro' or 'anti' sentiments at all, at least not in the polarized way in which we might want to view it.[13] Judaism was not monolithic, but full of diversity. Yet such insights, valuable as they undoubtedly were, often stopped short of assisting in the making sense of the Bible for the majority, and remained more or less within the confines of academic conferences, and upon library bookshelves. When they did venture into 'popular' discussion, the response was an awareness of *difference* rather than how this actually informed our rich heritage.

When I was an undergraduate one of my tutors frequently declared that 'context is king'. When studying a text, it is more common to think about its 'background', but the problem with that word is that it does what it says: it keeps many insights 'in the background'. 'Context' is a more engaging word, but it is also a word fraught with complexity. A. K. M. Adam speaks about 'contextual constellations', and this is a helpful image that implies that whatever the outcome of interpretation, it will not be 'one thing', and it will tell us as much about the interpreter as about the passage being interpreted.[14] How you see constellations very much depends on your location and perspective. How we gain meaning and appreciation of other ways of looking at texts, and all that means, relies upon our level of self-awareness. If we know something about the social context of the texts, they make more sense than if we did not take that into account in any way.

My own exposure to the discipline of social-scientific interpretation began when I was an undergraduate student at the University of St Andrews. One of my tutors (the same one who uttered the words above) was Philip Esler and it was he who introduced me to the work of The Context Group, which was formed in 1989. Two important publications by its founding members were *The New Testament World: Insights from Cultural Anthropology* (1981, second edition 1993) by Bruce J. Malina, and John H. Elliott's *Home for the Homeless: A Sociological Exegesis of 1 Peter* (also 1981). Elliott's 1993 publication *What is Social-Scientific Criticism of the Bible?* brought the group's methodology firmly into the academic arena.[15]

At the heart of social-scientific criticism is the assertion that in order to understand the texts of the Bible we need to free ourselves from our Western cultural assumptions, which inevitably obscure the meaning of the texts we are seeking to interpret. One of the key differences is that the modern Western world tends to be an individualistic, industrial society, whereas the society of the Mediterranean world was collectivistic and agrarian. Context Group work also drew attention to important cultural aspects such as honour and shame, purity and pollution, and the 'evil eye', all of which we cannot understand because we do not operate within the same culture as the texts of the Bible.[16] In his letter to the Galatians, Paul is so angry that he dispenses with the usual letter-writing protocol of beginning with a friendly greeting. Part of his exasperation with this community (who have apparently abandoned what Paul has taught them) results in his accusing them of possessing the 'evil eye' (3.1). Translations of the Greek vary, but many settle on something like 'Who has bewitched you?' This means nothing (much) to us, but when viewed in the social context of the passage, the serious nature of the 'evil eye' element of Paul's concern becomes clear, and moreover it has implications for how we read the letter as a whole.[17]

The work of social-scientific criticism impacted upon the Old Testament as well as the New, and brought fresh meaning to the contexts of its stories. In 1979 two important books appeared: Norman Gottwald's *The Tribes of Yahweh* and Robert Carroll's *When Prophecy Failed*.[18] Both employed insights from anthropology and sociology to enable us to better understand Israelite society and religion in the period 1250–1050 BCE. Other important books have appeared since those earlier developments, using the social sciences to investigate social roles such as prophet and king, honour and shame, and even gender.[19]

> There are important cultural aspects . . . that we cannot understand because we do not operate within the same culture

I well remember how the social-scientific approach opened up the texts to me in a way that was quite revolutionary to someone who had been firmly schooled in the techniques of historical criticism: asking questions of the texts in order to access their 'historical background'. Recognizing the Jewishness of both Jesus *and* Paul, and the variety within Judaism, linked discussion of context to identity, the defining of which marks a key feature of the biblical narrative, and one that is perhaps never finally resolved. For example, the complex relationship between the single Christian life and the larger community of the faithful is first articulated in an exploratory way by Paul in 1 Corinthians 12, but is by no means presented as the last word on the topic.[20]

When I began my graduate studies in the mid 1990s, I was convinced that social-scientific criticism held all the answers to making sense of the Bible. I did not foresee that I would find that assumption deeply challenged by an approach that asks the question 'So what?' While scholars are divided over one of the key aspects of social-scientific criticism, namely its use of anthropological models, perhaps the most pressing concern is how such insights can truly assist us in making sense of the texts if we cannot ourselves make sense of where we are.[21] Context *is* about acknowledging difference but it is also about sustaining willingness to journey together.[22] Is it possible, then, that insights from social-scientific criticism can accompany discussions of our own contexts? The answer is 'yes', but how we go about that is the continuing task of the development of other hermeneutical approaches that we shall explore shortly.

Perhaps one way of starting to explore this area is that the New Testament contains four versions of the same story, and this is illustrative of the observation in the previous chapter based on Richard Bauckham's work on eyewitnesses: that the evangelists are deeply *engaged* theologians and not just mouthpieces.[23] To make the link between their context and ours we need to know what 'our' context is – both where we are (thus context embraces the complexity of identity) and specifically, where we are *situated*. Whereas social-scientific approaches can assist us with making sense of the social location of the texts of the Bible, contextual and literary approaches can help with greater awareness of where *we* are and *how* we read texts.

A BBC online magazine article reported on how the developments in satellite navigation technology have raised fears that such systems are starting to erode local knowledge. The report also discussed how over-reliance on these mapping devices represents anxiety about the road and getting lost. More roads and better cars mean that we can travel further, and increases the likelihood that we might get lost somewhere along the way. More often than not, we are used to passing through places at speed, and the places we live in are very often just that, with no shared awareness of what roots the locality in which we are situated. Much of this, of course, relies upon perspective. As

I write, in my current southern hemisphere location, the moon appears to me to be upside down. Of course it's not, and a visitor from the southern hemisphere to the north would be equally valid in pronouncing the same assertion. The problem arises if I were to say that there is only one way of looking at the moon (the northern view) and that all other views must take their lead from my own perspective. It is true, then, that our location can define the limits of our interpretation, *or* it can expand those limits, thus opening new realms of possibility.[24]

The process of exploring our own contexts is called, not surprisingly, 'contextual hermeneutics', and this has itself given rise to a great number of 'cross-cultural' approaches.[25] Earlier we asserted how difference can be problematic or advantageous depending on how you approach it. Rather like the optimist/pessimist divide (is the glass half full or half empty?), difference can be the making or breaking of a community of faith. If different meanings are accepted and held in creative tension then progress can be made, but it all depends on how this is done and the willingness of the participants in interpretation to accept views that may be diametrically opposed to their own. We will explore more of this in Chapter 4 on 'Conversations', but it is worth reflecting on here as we discuss the contexts that we inhabit, lest they inhibit how we experience the richness that may be on offer to us.

Contextual Bible study

In *The Word in Place: Reading the New Testament in Contemporary Contexts*, Louise J. Lawrence introduces an approach known as 'contextual Bible study'. Originating in post-apartheid South Africa, this method gives priority to contextual community-based responses to biblical texts. This approach has been used in a great number of biblical studies that have emerged particularly in a post-colonial context, and has resulted in powerful reflections on how the texts function in contexts that seek deeper meaning from them. It further allows for dialogue *between* contexts, acknowledging difference in cultural values but affirmation in the continuity of meaning between the 'then' and the 'now'. Lawrence's own study focused on communities in Cornwall, England, and demonstrated how recovery of a sense of 'place' can lend itself to a more fruitful engagement with texts. 'Place' does not refer to a romantic or idealized notion of 'where we are' but constantly searches for ways in which stories can contribute to constructive dialogues and challenge positions of interpretative stance where necessary.[26]

Throughout this chapter, we have reflected on how differences in context can bring us together or drive us apart. By way of illustrating how I have experienced this at first hand, I once led a seminar on the Apostle Paul's missionary strategy with a group of Maori clergy from a northern diocese in Aotearoa New Zealand. Part of my reflections focused upon how Paul seems to wrestle with the tension between the 'global' and 'local' nature of his task. In Romans 1.8 Paul highlights the 'global' impetus behind the declaration of the gospel – 'because your faith is proclaimed throughout the world' – and in 1 Corinthians he asserts the theological importance of the 'local': 'Do you not know that you [plural] are God's temple and that God's Spirit dwells in you? If anyone destroys God's temple, God will destroy that person. For God's temple is holy.'[27] Of course, these quotations are drawn from two different letters, written to two different locations at different points in Paul's career. The point is made clear enough, however, that this dynamic of a faith that is much greater than one specific location, and a faith that is inevitably expressed with local 'colour', lies at the heart of the texts of the Bible and even more so as they provide the foundational documents of the Christian faith. It was only when I had displayed a map of the location of Corinth that those I was with began to discuss with some enthusiasm the connections between the geography of Corinth (located on an isthmus) and that of the city of Auckland (likewise situated), and the social, religious and political points that I had made with regard to Paul's context could gain meaning in the light of an explicit awareness of the 'present' context of those participating in the Bible study.

This example of the working out of context is naturally a very specific one, and would not lend itself to that type of direct comparison elsewhere (not all cities are located on an isthmus), but in that particular context it led to immediate engagement. Suddenly a letter written long ago spoke afresh into a present-day context. A crucial aspect of this was knowledge about the local. This may be an obvious point, but

Suddenly a letter written long ago spoke afresh into a present-day context

as we explored earlier, without the local knowledge-base, we have less to go by when it comes to making sense of the Bible.

This chapter has discussed the importance of contexts in our task of making sense of the Bible. Along with an appreciation of the story-based setting of the texts of the Bible, an awareness of context begins to add colour and texture to the many ways in which we engage with the Bible today. In the next chapter, we look at the encounters that we have with the Bible that can assist (or indeed obscure) our making sense of the stories and the contexts that we have examined and how we might negotiate our way along the hermeneutical pathway.

3

Encounters

'Have you sat?'

So far on our journey we have reflected on the importance of attending to the texts of the Bible in their 'literal' sense, and of us being 'considerate readers', aware of how contexts affect the meaning of the texts and our ability to access those meanings where we are. This chapter focuses on the theme of 'encounters', exploring different types of encounter, and ponders what this might be able to teach us about how we encounter the texts of the Bible. Part of our task, too, will be to examine some of the key interpretative tools that have been developed to assist our reading of the texts, if only to conclude that any one critical tool alone is never enough. We bring ourselves to the texts and in so doing we must be able to allow our own stories to gain meaning through the inner life of the texts themselves. Such an assertion is not an especially popular one in the field of the academic study of the Bible, but it is an honest one if we are to make sense of what the Bible is to us, wherever we might be.

> We must be able to allow our own stories to gain meaning through the inner life of the texts themselves

The history of biblical interpretation contains a great variety of approaches to the texts, some of which were discussed in the previous chapter on contexts. Social-scientific and contextual

46

interpretations have as their main aim the desire to make clear how differences in context can bring about a clearer reflection on meaning in the present. In order to do this, our context must be acknowledged and consciously borne in mind when we read the texts; only then can we sustain the willingness to journey together with the differences that the texts may illuminate. The danger, of course, is that texts can become overly 'domesticated', and their meaning ultimately held in place in a way that can become too rigid. However, if texts are held in community (whatever that 'community' might be), then individualism is held in balance with the collective identity of the 'body of Christ'.

The question posed at the beginning of this chapter – 'Have you sat?' – relates to the work of performance artist Marina Abramović, *The Artist is Present*, which was on display in the Museum of Modern Art in New York City from 14 March to 31 May 2010. The work involved Abramović sitting at a plain wooden table with an empty chair opposite. Members of the public (and celebrities, of course), took their turn at sitting down opposite her; the celebrities were usually given the opportunity to 'jump the line'. After one particular gentleman (and would-be performance artist) spent six hours sitting, the time period allowed was reduced to a ten-minute allocation per person. Abramović managed to stare 1,500 people in the face over the course of 700 hours of performance. Her show was seen by half a million people, outperforming the other major exhibition at the time, of work by the film-maker Tim Burton. Not surprisingly, reactions varied between extreme dislike at the apparent pointlessness of what she was doing 'in the name of art' to those in a state of quasi-religious hysteria. My own reaction was somewhere in between. I spent a good amount of time one day watching the whole performance from a balcony area above. It is hard to describe the fullness of what it was I was looking at, and why indeed I spent such a long time just looking. I bumped into a friend who had spent the sum total of five minutes in the whole gallery, never mind just that particular area, and couldn't wait to get out. It seems that modern art often inspires people to reactions of almost instant like and dislike. Whatever was going on in that space, it was one of the most vivid examples that I had ever seen of what an encounter could be like. Yes, it was staged, and I acknowledge that many encounters that we have are rather more accidental, but there was something about what I was looking at that demanded I just do that – look – and from that questions began to emerge about what I was seeing. There was an inner life to the performance that was unfolding over time.[1]

This example of an encounter suggests that there is always more to be gained in meaning than that which results from just describing what lies in front of us. People who sat opposite Marina Abramović did not speak to her, but a common response was the shedding of tears. Any text that we encounter and may startle or puzzle us will not give us all the answers straight away, and even if we approach the text with a particular mode of interpretation, our understanding at any given moment will always be partial, and we will keep on striving to know and understand more. We touched on this briefly in the Introduction, when we reflected on how awareness of the diversity of stories in the Bible makes us want to know more deeply what they mean, and this is a process sometimes referred to as the 'hermeneutical spiral'. It is not a spiral into infinity, however, but a spiral that is constantly being renewed.[2] It moves outwards, it does not collapse in on itself.

In an article entitled 'How to give Hamlet's "to be or not to be" new meaning', Tom Geoghegan explores the difficulties involved with breathing new life into the well-known Shakespearean drama. In particular, Geoghegan reflects on the famous 'To be or not to be' passage which comes in Act III Scene 1, when Prince Hamlet is trying to establish his uncle's guilt in murdering his father and usurping the Danish throne. The scene is much more than a sequence of words; it is 'a deep philosophical reflection on life and death'.[3] In the article the theatre critic Michael Billington is quoted saying that 'the challenge is to make the audience listen to what Hamlet is saying, rather than drift into a hazy memory of school days. They need to sit up and listen to this man who is debating whether to kill himself or not to kill himself and why by the end he decides not to.' The actor Samuel West, who spent a year playing Hamlet in 2001, observes that interpretations can differ, depending on how much you think Hamlet is suicidal or philosophical. There is also a choice between introspection and engagement, how much the actor 'looks the audience in the eye'.

With the stories of the Bible, there are many that are perhaps overly familiar to us, and many that are not. One of the more familiar stories is that describing the birth of Jesus, but the average nativity play will not adhere to either Matthew's or Luke's version of the story, but will likely collapse the whole narrative into one story, with other details thrown in for good measure. It is not unusual to find a whole zoo of animals crowding out the manger scene, and an almost exhausting line of shepherds and magi visitors lining up to see Jesus. If that becomes the way the story is encountered, then what happens to the integrity of the Gospel narratives? It is a tricky path to negotiate. As we saw earlier, it is possible for meaning to become interrupted, for stories to take on a life that is somewhere outside the confines of the text. This can make for an uncomfortable

> **It is possible for meaning to become interrupted**

encounter, or it can be an opportunity to re-engage with the story in a 'literal' sense. There was something of this in the BBC's efforts to make the events of the birth and death of Jesus more contemporary a few years ago.[4]

Just occasionally, the opportunity arises to encounter a whole book (or near enough) of the Bible on stage, in a 'literal' sense. George Dillon's critically acclaimed performance of *The Gospel of Matthew* enables the text of that Gospel to come to life in a most remarkable way, bringing new meaning to the stories contained in it. Dillon begins not at the point we might expect him to, with the birth of Jesus, but where the Gospel itself begins: with the genealogy of Jesus in Matthew 1. Finding meaning in genealogies takes more than just developing an ability to pronounce tricky names, however; it is about appreciating the layers of stories that these names bring to the text, stories that are implicit rather than explicitly mentioned. Close attention to Matthew's list reveals names such as Tamar (Genesis 38), Rahab (Joshua 2), Ruth, and Bathsheba (named as 'the wife of Uriah' in Matthew 1.6; 2 Samuel 11 and 12). Matthew intends for his readers to be alert to the significant implications of these women as part of Jesus' lineage; these women's stories contain details that others would want to 'airbrush' out of the picture. A feminist interpretation could approach this positively or negatively, asking questions of the Gospel text but perhaps more pointedly about

> These women's stories contain details that others would want to 'airbrush' out of the picture

the negative stereotyping of so-called 'loose women' in the narratives themselves. Such questions aside, Dillon's performance of the Gospel is a useful reminder that these are texts which to a great extent make sense in an overtly dramatic way; the challenge is how to make such stories more contemporary, as with the Manchester Passion and Liverpool Nativity, or whether indeed that is absolutely necessary in order to gain meaning.[5] Is an encounter with the text 'as it is' what we should be aiming at?

This suggests that an over-focus on making the Bible 'contemporary' can in fact result in diminishing the 'literal' sense of the stories. Yet we often shy away from an encounter with the 'literalness' of the texts. We can read them, but we really wouldn't want to actually *be* there, would we? Any encounter with the texts of the Bible should be thought*ful* and rooted in our particularity as children of God, allowing our weakness to be held by God's overwhelming grace. Each one of us ought to be passionate about communicating the Bible, and about exploring fresh ways of allowing it to speak into our own contexts to inform our readings, bringing to light values that are contained within the texts but do not always have a voice. This is not an especially new endeavour; just take the issue of slavery, and the way in which appreciation for the slave as fellow human being became a crucial part of the journey towards emancipation in the nineteenth century. Interpretation of texts that seem un-negotiable in fact produces endless negotiation in order to allow fresh meaning to emerge.[6]

Any texts written down, gathered together, and given authority by a community are subject to criticism. Biblical criticism (also known as hermeneutics) arguably began even before the Bible was assembled in its canonical form. Part of the complexity in understanding how hermeneutics operates lies in our understanding of it as a dual process that is both *descriptive* as method and *philosophical* in its theological assumptions. In other words hermeneutics, the formal process by which we try to gather meaning from a text, relies on the following of certain methodological rules (depending on which particular category of interpretation you are trying to adhere to). It also very much draws upon a whole series of assumptions that lie behind the actions of the person doing the interpreting, assumptions that depend very much on the theological understandings brought to the text and that are often never explicitly acknowledged. Encounters can be risky and can place us in vulnerable positions. When Marina Abramović finished her 'sitting', her biggest thank you was reserved for the security guard who had accompanied her for the whole performance. At that point it became clear how vulnerable she must have felt.

In her edited volume *Searching for Meaning: An Introduction to Interpreting the New Testament*,[7] Paula Gooder gathers together 23 different types of interpretative approach. The book is divided into three categories: *event to text* (exploring the journey from the original text to its final written form); *text* (the desire to understand better the final form of a text, as we have it); and *from text to reader* (examining the relationship between the text and its readers). Critical perspectives ranging from historical criticism, narrative criticism, to post-colonial criticism and ecological criticism are given thorough treatment from experts in these areas. Weaving throughout, though not explicitly addressed, are hotly debated questions such as, 'Is the original meaning of the text ever accessible?' While these approaches can produce meaning from the texts, part of the difficulty is enabling these meanings (whatever they may be) to be truly relevant and interesting and indeed to be 'in conversation' with each other. This is where conversations are a vital part of the process, and we shall be returning to that topic in Chapter 4 as we draw together the various strands that we have been exploring throughout the course of this book. There are four approaches in particular that are worth exploring in brief here, as they have been both foundational and highly influential in developing our understanding of the texts, albeit with varying degrees of success and accessibility.

Four approaches

Historical criticism is made up of a number of approaches that are aimed at assisting our understanding of the 'world of the text'. These approaches tell us much about the development of critical thought in general, particularly from the period of the eighteenth-century Enlightenment onwards, with advances in other areas of study such as translation, anthropology, ethnography and archaeology. The result of developments in historical criticism was a rise in the *description* of the world of the texts.

Form criticism brought its focus to the *literary* aspects of the texts: the patterns and 'typical' features of story-types (in the New Testament, miracles and parables in the Gospels, for example). This critical approach was in fact first applied to the Old Testament by the German scholar Hermann Gunkel (1862–1932), who adapted 'folklore studies' to the biblical texts, drawing in particular on the work of the Brothers Grimm, who assembled a collection of German folktales during the nineteenth century. Gunkel's aim was to examine each story-unit (known as a pericope, a word we encountered earlier in Chapter 1) and connect it to a historical situation. Particularly influential has been his classification of the Psalms as 'hymns', 'communal laments', 'individual laments', 'individual thanks-giving songs', and 'royal psalms'. When it comes to the New Testament, the early twentieth-century scholars Martin Dibelius and Rudolf Bultmann are synonymous with the application of this critical approach, much of which was focused upon the Gospels and the life of Jesus in particular. This coincided with developments in the so-called 'quest for the historical Jesus': the desire and belief that it was possible to access information that would lead to the historical character about which the Gospels spoke.

Source criticism, as its name suggests, involved identification of the literary sources used in the construction of biblical narratives. For the Old Testament, the identification of the sources known as J [Yahwist], E [Elohist], P [Priestly] and D [Deuteronomist] proved highly influential; in New Testament studies the application of source criticism has rested almost entirely on attempts to solve the 'synoptic problem', with its questions of how to account for the similarities and differences between the Gospels of Mark, Matthew and Luke.

Redaction criticism focuses more upon the role of the authors in editing their material together. Or rather, more than editing: the choosing, arranging, expanding and leaving out of material. Much of this approach has had its focus on the Gospels (again), and an especially influential example of this type of critical approach may be seen in the German scholar Günther Bornkamm's article 'The Stilling of the Storm in Matthew', which examined how the changes Matthew makes to Mark's account reflect the situation of the church community for whom Matthew was writing.[8]

These four critical approaches form the basis of most types of interpretation today, even if those interpretations react against the premises they contain rather than necessarily build on the assumptions they present. The challenge to find meaning in texts using these and other approaches that may or may not be ultimately helpful is reflective of a broad tension within the Bible itself, the tension between just 'being' in God's eternal nature and actually 'doing', which is what the prophets in the Old Testament (Isaiah 51.9–11), John the Baptist (Mark 1.1–8) and the Apostle Paul (Romans 13.11–12) urge us to do: Wake up! Pay attention! This doesn't mean staying awake while someone talks at us; rather it is a cry to simply get on with the stuff of life in all its ordinariness and messiness – which is precisely what the incarnation was, and is, about. Christians believe that through the cross and resurrection, God affirmed a hope in humanity that brought us through the shadow of death into an eternal light. Remember, even shadows need light.

How did we get here?

Encounters can create in us the strong desire to reflect: to consider and indeed reconsider the questions of our life journeys, such as, 'How did we get here?' and 'What does it mean?' It is an opportunity to wait on God, to learn *how* to wait, and perhaps most importantly of all, to think about what we are waiting for. The hermeneutical process truly is one that in order to be fully engaged must enable the asking of questions that may well be considered more explicitly philosophical in nature.

Part of the challenge of any encounter is the creating of space within which object and mystery might come together to encounter God's eternity; the point of encounter creates the opportunity for change. The prophet Isaiah describes what happens when this space is galvanized into being (51.6):

> Raise your eyes to the heavens, look down at the earth; for the heavens will vanish like smoke, the earth wear out like clothing and its inhabitants die like vermin, but my salvation will last for ever and my saving justice remain inviolable.   (NJB)

Isaiah's heralding cry does not stem from an overactive imagination; it is an assertion that time and history are the plains upon which God is working out his purposes. The resurrection displayed that sense of connection between human frailty and its redemption in a truly wondrous way. Our lives are *lived*, actively,

> Isaiah's heralding cry . . . is an assertion that time and history are the plains upon which God is working out his purposes

against the backdrop of God's presence, leading us forward, pulling us forward in history, not just spiralling out of control. Every day is a day drawing closer to God: our salvation *is* 'nearer than when we first began to believe' (as Paul writes in Romans 13.11). The prophet's words are not meant to inspire fear, but rather hope and encouragement in our encounters.

Like objects in a museum, we are rooted in past events that have shaped us and made us who we are. We all come from the local, or the particular; but the gospel message invites us, challenges us even, to be rooted collectively in the body of Christ. It is this hope that anticipates the resurrection, that connects our rootedness with eternity, that challenges our humanity out of complacency towards accountability.

On a recent bus journey home, during a pause at traffic lights I glanced to my left and looked at the windows of Science Oxford, which aims to promote public understanding of the wonders of science. Through the glass I could see a group of schoolchildren excitedly trying one of the many 'hands-on' experiments. What really caught my eye, however, were the words painted all over the windows: explore, curious, involve, passion, enjoy, interact, exchange, discover, question, debate, society, understand, together.

It would be interesting to imagine such words used of our encounters with the texts of the Bible. I don't wish to sound naive, but there is much in the state of current debates involving the Bible that is deeply concerning, in unthinking and uncritical interpretations of texts. After all, there should be room for debate and disagreement while still allowing for God's overwhelming grace to remind us that any encounter should involve humility, generosity and graciousness.

Encounters don't just take place between ourselves and the texts; indeed, many stories in the Bible are themselves results of encounters (the story of the Apostle Paul stems entirely from his encounter with the risen Jesus on the road to Damascus, as recounted in Acts, to cite just one example). The outcome of interpretation can limp, like Jacob wrestling with what cannot be named in Genesis 32. There is always considerably more to be discussed and understood.[9] Any interpretation carries with it a legacy that must be explained and constantly rewritten so that meaning is not lost. This would be especially true of the particular critical approaches identified earlier. Although foundational, they are by no means exclusive or even relevant in their capacity to hold meaning for us today.

To a certain extent this chapter has been a transitional one in our search for meaning. Encounter alone cannot bring meaning and sense to the Bible, and indeed, part of the difficulty with critical approaches, particularly those developed under the umbrella of Christianity, is that they almost exclusively ignore other aspects of our heritage, namely Jewish interpretation. As it turns out, this latter area contains considerable insights that may inform and challenge what we have discovered so far. This conversational approach, which holds together both imagination and incredible attention to detail, may be the key that we need to unlock the sense of the Bible in the fullest way possible. To return to the performance work of Marina Abramović mentioned at the start of this chapter, one wonders what would have happened if she had spoken with those who sat opposite her, instead of just staring at them. The usual reverential silence of a gallery space filled with the noise of conversation. Then what?

4

Conversations

———•◆•———

'. . . live in fragments no longer'

(E. M. Forster, *Howards End*)

In July 2009 the Gallery of Modern Art in Glasgow caused considerable controversy with an exhibition entitled 'Made in God's Image'. A copy of the Bible was put on display next to a container of pens, accompanied by a notice saying: 'If you feel you have been excluded from the Bible, please write your way back into it.' Not surprisingly, many of the comments that were written were motivated by a desire to deface rather than to engage (at least that was the interpretation provided by the media). Following the outcry, the Bible remained on display in a glass case, and members of the public were invited to write their comments in another book alongside. One critic said that the offensive material was 'symbolic of the state of our broken and lawless society . . . the Bible stands for everything this art does not: for creation, beauty, hope and regeneration'. When asked about this controversial piece, the artist commented: 'If we are to open up the Bible for discussion, surely we have to invite people to speak out . . . art allows us to discuss difficult things.'[1] There can be no doubt that this exhibition was provocative, but somehow the response of the critic that the Bible stands for everything the art apparently did not – 'creation, beauty, hope and regeneration' – imposes a narrative arc on the texts that does not take account of the complexities of that narrative and does not engage with the parts of the Bible that we would rather ignore, given half the chance. How, one might well ask, does the story of gang-rape and dismemberment in Judges 19 tell of beauty and hope?[2]

We have already encountered the words of the quotation cited above, taken from E. M. Forster's novel *Howards End*. The book is about three families in England at the beginning of the twentieth century. The three families represent different parts of the Edwardian middle class: the Wilcoxes, who are rich capitalists with a fortune made in the colonies, the half-German Schlegel siblings who are members of the intellectual bourgeoisie, and the Basts, a couple who are struggling members of the lower middle class. The Schlegel sisters try to help the Basts and try to make the Wilcoxes less prejudiced. The motto of the book is 'only connect', found in the sentence immediately preceding the quotation above.[3] Forster's novel was highly influential upon the more recent *On Beauty* by Zadie Smith.[4] *Howards End* begins with the sentence, 'One may as well begin with Helen's letters to her sister'; *On Beauty* with, 'One may as well begin with Jerome's e-mails to his father'. Although the two books are not directly in conversation with each other, they are in a dialogue of sorts, and both books are entertaining and provocative. The desire to 'live in fragments no longer', voiced in *Howards End*, becomes a reflective lens through which the intricacies of human relationships are explored by Smith in her novel. Conversations are often powerful, brief, haphazard and deeply meaningful, sometimes all at once. The pages upon which the narratives unfold are full of life in all its rawness and richness, with the potential for the journey to turn in unexpected directions ever present.

In much the same way, the narrative of the texts of the Bible unfolds as we attend to the 'literalness' of the stories. Making sense of the Bible involves opening up a hermeneutical space that allows conversations and connections to be made. Part of that process may involve the use of certain interpretative tools, as we have already discussed. Yet hermeneutics isn't enough on its own. Sooner or later there is a need to move to a deeper engagement with what the whole process might be telling us about God and about ourselves in relation to God and to each other. It is all very well sharing interpretation and meaning, but what happens when we understand each other better – then what?[5] The answer, perhaps simply, is that conversations often have a life of their own and they continue, 'off the page', sometimes unscripted and constantly taking on potential for new meaning. Indeed, often those conversations will involve the telling of stories, experiences and personal insights that may illuminate meaning ever further. This is not an especially new endeavour, but rather is rich within our Judaeo-Christian heritage, as we shall explore shortly.

Part of the difficulty in making sense of the Bible is the way in which 'the text' often presents us with one side of a conversation. Sometimes this is quite literally the case, as with the letters in the New Testament; at other times there is a more general awareness of voices outside the texts, or voices in the texts that are silent. This is not an end to meaning; it just requires awareness and sensitivity to the ways in which the texts are themselves 'unfinished'. At the same time, of course, the Bible is full of conversations, and of texts in conversation with each other, often in subtle ways. Alongside all of these conversations are the ways in which we contribute to the ongoing conversation, even in ways that may be inherently risky or perhaps controversial, as in the example of the Glasgow exhibition described above. Yet as Walter Brueggemann observes, 'if we do not keep the conversation going with the script, we shall all be scripted in ways that are neither human nor faithful'.[6]

In Chapter 1 we discussed the ways in which our own stories could be told into and alongside the stories of the Bible to give both meaning. Another way of expressing this is to say that our stories are the 'midrash' to the literal 'plain' text. In Jewish rabbinic exegesis midrashim (the plural of midrash) are the interpretational conversations that the rabbis have to try and make sense of the texts. The word 'midrash'

> Our stories are the 'midrash' to the literal 'plain' text of the stories in the Bible

is itself derived from the verb *darash*, meaning 'to seek'. If we take this broad sense of meaning of the word, then the earliest midrashim can be found in the Old Testament (the Hebrew Bible) itself. The books of 1 and 2 Chronicles have been considered as midrash on 1 and 2 Kings, 1 and 2 Samuel, and the 'P' (Priestly) document of the Torah (the first five books of the Bible).[7] Midrash is also identified within the New Testament, at Galatians 3.16 for example, which could be considered as midrash on Genesis 12.7 and 13.15. G. W. Buchanan has suggested that the book of Hebrews is midrash on Psalm 110.[8]

More formal rabbinic midrashim are collected in two categories: 'midrash halakhah', consisting of legal exposition on Exodus through to Deuteronomy, and 'midrash haggadah', consisting of narrative exposition.[9] Midrashic interpretation consists of a quotation of an Old Testament verse followed by commentary that might include devotional comments, personal stories and explanatory notes, often by different rabbinic voices. Exposition generally follows specific rabbinical rules of interpretation but is not restricted to these rules. There is meticulous attention to detail, combined with an imaginative and creative freedom that constantly refreshes and energizes the texts under discussion. In *Genesis Rabbah*, for example, the author discusses the first letter of the first word in Genesis 1.1, *bereshit*: 'Why was the world created with a b? . . . Because it connotes a blessing.'[10]

Rabbinic interpretation thus allows for the use of creativity and imagination to shed meaning upon the texts. Alexander Deeg, in 'Imagination and Meticulousness: *Haggadah* and *Halakhah* in Judaism and Christian Preaching', cites the example of the story of Jacob's ladder in Genesis 28.10–19 in its rabbinical interpretation.[11] As the story goes, Jacob lies down at the end of the day to rest. He places a rock under his head and goes to sleep, and he dreams of a ladder ascending to heaven with angels all around it. Jacob wakes and names the place where he has been sleeping 'God's house' (*Bethel*). Commentators on this story often focus on how the story gives meaning to the place name; that is its purpose. This is interesting, of course, but is by no means the only line of meaning that the story provides, and the rabbis recognize that there is more to the text than just what is written on the page. To this end, the rabbis discover things within the text that make them want to delve even deeper into its meaning. This attention to minute detail is demonstrated in the observation that the angels 'ascend and descend', when shouldn't they be doing the opposite – appearing from above, from the heavens, and then descending to the earth? Does this detail mean that the angels were there with Jacob all the time? The answer is 'yes'. This example makes it clear that attention to detail is of the greatest importance, and that this requires the type of slow reading of the story that we explored in Chapter 1. Attention to the literal sense of the text allows for imagination to fill the hermeneutical space created. There is not *one* correct meaning but rather endless potentials of meaning.

> Attention to the literal sense of the text allows for imagination to fill the hermeneutical space created

Another way of exploring further this insight is with the rabbinical tradition of 'black fire on white fire'. This phrase comes from the 'midrash Tan-huma', a group of texts that were collected together between the years 400 and 600: 'The Torah is full of holy fire; it was written with a black fire upon a white fire.'

The black fire refers to the letters of Torah, the actual words written down. The white refers to the spaces in between the letters. Together, black and white make up the whole of Torah. On another level, the black fire represents the literal meaning of the text, and the white fire represents ideas that we bring to the text when we read it. The white fire has endless potential for new meaning that can incorporate stories, songs, even silence, when meaning cannot be found in its fullness (yet). If you look at a rabbinic scroll, the black text is always completely surrounded by white parchment, and in fact this is laid down as an instruction in the Talmud: black fire must always be surrounded by white fire.[12]

It is important to assert at this juncture that midrash and other rabbinic rules of interpretation are not free and limit-less exercises (though meaning contains an endless potential of meaning); they are firmly grounded in certain principles and procedures that are well documented.[13] There are, for example, the 'seven rules of Hillel' (from the rabbinic interpretative school of the first century BCE which lasted until the fifth century CE), and the 'thirteen rules of Rabbi Ishmael' (from some time before the third century CE which expand on Hillel's seven rules). When it comes to midrash, however, there is an argument that this is more of a religious activity (in the sense that it derives from an active verb, 'to seek') and thus the rules of biblical interpretation are not restricted to the hermeneutical rules mentioned above. The rabbis on the one hand believe that everything is in Torah (it is complete) and yet they remain ever aware that Scripture is often full of ambiguity and that this is often given meaning by the white fire.

This way of interweaving stories with interpretation of texts is used by Jesus in the parables. 'Parable' is, of course, a term loaded with a good deal of theological and scholarly baggage (as David Stern discusses in his study of midrash and parables).

> **The interweaving of stories with interpretation of texts is used by Jesus in the parables**

Stern points out that a parable (with its cognate Hebrew form, *mashal*) is 'an allusive narrative told for an ulterior purpose'.[14] Daniel Boyarin holds that midrash (like all interpretation) involves the filling in of gaps in the narrative text. The gap itself is, as Boyarin points out:

> a complex concept, which essentially means any place in the text that requires the intervention of the reader to make sense of the story. Gap filling . . . involves the application of cultural knowledge, i.e., the mobilization of narrative schemata which are in the repertoire or sociolect of the culture in question.[15]

It is into this 'gap' that the conversation takes place in search of meaning. So when Jesus brings meaning to a situation he often does this through the telling of a story (parable) which one assumes would resonate with his audience, who in turn might be expected to contribute their own experiences to the interpretative conversation. Interestingly, it has been suggested that the most famous parables in the Jesus tradition (such as those of the prodigal son in Luke 15.11–32 and the good Samaritan in Luke 10.25–37) may have been stories that took several hours to tell, and that what we have are 'plot summaries'.[16]

One suggestion that follows from this recognition that there may be *more* to the text than first meets the eye is that our own lives in their incompleteness mirror the texts. Our own stories are constantly being put together and re-put together in a similar way to those of the Church, which is itself a community of interpretative practice. This matches what we explored about stories in Chapter 1 and in particular the assertion of the need for a more 'narrative'-like approach to understanding our own lives and the ways in which we can search for meaning in the texts of the Bible. The idea that Jesus 'performed' (for want of a better word) his teaching (parables and the like) reminds us that as they were first encountered these were texts that were bound to have produced conversations about their content, aspects of which may have included the use of 'local' understanding, idiom, even dialect.

In her book *Marking Time: Preaching Biblical Stories in Present Tense*,[17] Barbara K. Lundblad tells a wonderfully amusing autobiographical story of how she was preparing to write a sermon on Jesus' teaching in Matthew 19.24: 'It is easier for a camel to go through the eye of a needle, than for a rich man to enter the Kingdom of God.' She describes a scene outside a busy shopping area where a man stood, begging. Shoppers went in and out of a food market, collecting groceries and takeaway coffees, and the man remained largely ignored. Her own dilemma revolved around what to do, and she comments: 'Jesus taps us on the shoulder, and he's got this camel.' It's a wonderfully evocative image, comical even, and yet powerfully performative (you can *imagine* it happening). One wonders whether, even in its original setting, the first hearers of this teaching would have reflected on its comic potential: a camel through the eye of a needle, really? Lundblad reflects that there are 'two parts to the interpretative conversation: the text marks our time, and our time marks the text. Only when both are remembered and honoured can God's untameable texts find meaning in the midst of our changing lives.'[18]

She continues: 'our task is not to update the Bible, but to open up a hermeneutical space in which life itself serves to explain the text, a space in which time and text are in lively conversation with each other'.[19] This resonates, too, with the rabbinic way of interpreting texts, the idea of 'opening up a hermeneutical space' into which conversations can be had to find meaning;

not that that meaning may be left disparate and chaotic, however, but rather like the fragments gathered up in the miracle of the feeding of the 5,000 (Matthew 14.13–21; Mark 6.31–44; Luke 9.10–17; John 6.5–15) there is always more to be gained from what first meets the eye in the text. Jesus instructs the disciples to gather up the fragments in order to show how much more there was than first imagined. We return again to the E. M. Forster quotation we encountered in the Introduction: 'Only connect the prose and the passion and both will be exalted, and human love will be seen at its height. Live in fragments no longer.'

The textual example that concludes this chapter draws together the 'fragments' of this book in its reflection on the themes of story, context, encounter and conversation, and the way in which these together 'make sense' of the Bible. That

> How we encounter a text very much depends on our perspective

is not to suggest, of course, that meaning is final or fixed. Ultimately, the journey of discipleship is ongoing and open for each one of us, something that the Gospel itself asserts. How we encounter a text very much depends on our perspective.

Textual example from the New Testament: Mark 1.1 (and 16.8)[20]

Often when we arrive somewhere new, or begin a new job or stage in life, we reflect on the journey that took us to that place. It is what we are programmed to do, to reflect *back* to make sense of the present reality.

At the very least, however, we should give a nod in the direction of 'historical context' in how we both describe and understand time. Many scholars have spoken of the importance of acknowledging the *eschatological* context of the first century.

Christopher Rowland writes that 'for Jews, the promise of a final vindication of the Jewish people and the establishment of a new order in which God's ways would prevail was a belief which had its roots in the covenant relationship itself (2 Sam. 7.8f.)'.[21]

The Gospel that perhaps best encapsulates the sense of urgency behind that 'eschatological' milieu is Mark. He begins his Gospel with the prophetic character John the Baptist, who bursts on the scene announcing that the time is *now*, the place is *here* and the purpose is *this*. The time has arrived, the rule of God is at hand; trust this proclamation. It is essentially an announcement that God is taking over!

What is so exciting is the way in which Mark carefully crafts his narrative so as to help his readers (and that includes us) to address the tenses of past and present for the meaning of faith: 'How did I get here, and what does it mean?' This, for Mark, is why the theme of discipleship seeps out of every word in his Gospel and engages with us in our present contexts.

Mark begins his Gospel by declaring: 'Beginning of the good news (Gospel) of Jesus Messiah Son of God'. That very first word is a rendering of the Greek *arche* (there's no word for 'the' – it's straight in: 'beginning'). Mark deliberately gives the word 'beginning' a wide meaning, implying, I suggest, that the *ending* may not be in the text at all but in the life of the hearer. This is particularly interesting if we follow the argument that Mark's Gospel finishes abruptly at 16.8, without the neat ending of the other Gospels. More on that topic of 'ending' shortly.

Second, the '*good news of* Jesus Christ' is ambiguous: Christ is both the subject and the object of the 'good news'. Mark wants believers, as they wrestle with the discipleship question (How did I get here, and what does it mean?) to stand at the point of two moments, two tenses: *imagining* what it was like for Jesus to hear John's message and to respond to his call to baptism; and *knowing* that he (Jesus) was the one who fulfilled the greater promise of baptism with the Holy Spirit.

This is an invitation for the hearers to place themselves at the outset in the journey through Mark, to hear this story as the emergence of the origins of their own discipleship and its meaning; encountering the text gives rise to the search for meaning through (one may well suggest) conversation. The hearers' appreciation of this point is further enhanced in 1.7 where we may discern something dramatic in Mark's use of tenses, moving between the *past* ('he started proclaiming') and *future* promise ('the stronger-one-than-me is coming after me . . .'), with the *present* continuous participle ('saying').

> We may discern something dramatic in Mark's use of tenses

The whole narrative has a dramatic import, as if on the cusp of something that is uniting Jesus and believers together: Jesus hearing these words for the first time, and believers hearing Jesus hear these words for the first time, and so finding encouragement through the story they are about to hear, which is the whole of Mark's Gospel. They and Jesus are together 'in at the beginning' of the narrative. This motif is a hallmark of the whole of Mark's Gospel.

So this is actually a key dramatic moment that involves for both Jesus' hearers and Mark's readers something about discipleship that is indeed about the 'significance of beginning, continuing and arriving', and resonating with that key human learning experience of 'How did I get here, and what does it mean?' If we keep this in mind, we can gain much in our reading of Mark's Gospel: how he frames his narrative with this broad theme of discipleship (as journeying with Christ, and as relating to those around us as part of the body of Christ).

But what of the ending? The Scottish crime writer Ian Rankin was once asked about his novels, which typically don't end in a neat and tidy fashion. One story in particular finishes with two of the main characters having a conversation 'off the page'. Rankin explained that his American publisher found this unacceptable, and he had to write an extra chapter for the US edition. But why end with a conversation that we cannot read and only imagine? Life's just not like that, was his reply; rarely do things end neatly, with all the 'i's dotted and the 't's crossed. That, in a sense, is where the Easter story fits in. There was death and there was resurrection, but then what? Is it an ending, or a beginning, or both?

The women come to the tomb, the stone has been rolled back, and as they enter they see a young man who tells them not to be alarmed; Jesus has been raised and they are to tell Jesus' disciples and Peter that they will meet Jesus in Galilee. The women flee, 'for terror and amazement had seized them; and they said nothing to anyone, for they were afraid' (16.8).

Our Gospel writer, Mark, writes because he wants to tell Jesus' story to a community facing persecution and death – which may be why he spends half of his Gospel describing the events surrounding Jesus' dying. He needs (surely) to get the story right, to tell what he knows so convincingly that someone coming afterwards will not forget the story, but will find its truth and make it their own. There is only one problem with this. If your challenge was to get the story right, to create a record so compelling that others would come to faith by it, you wouldn't leave the story the way Mark does – or would you? As Romeo said to Juliet after their first meeting, 'Wouldst thou leave me so unsatisfied?'

Well, that's what Mark does to us. Maybe there's wisdom in Mark's narrative. After all, how would you explain the resurrection to a smart, savvy crowd today? There were no cameras, no 24-hour rolling news bulletins. And what, if anything, might there have been anyway that wouldn't be subject to interpretation? Give the story of Easter to Matthew, Luke or John and they have none of Mark's reticence. They tell of resurrection appearances aplenty. But Mark leaves us with the women at the tomb glued to the spot with fear and amazement. They aren't shivering in their sandals, however; they react in much the same way as any character in the biblical narratives does to a divine revelation – they are full not of weak fear but of awe-filled wonder.

But I wonder why Mark leaves it this way. Clearly this caused a bit of a debate in the early Church, which is why we have a number of different, longer endings to the Gospel. Some have suggested that something must have been lost – a theologically keen 'Easter bunny' nibbled the last page of the manuscript. Or is Mark just teasing us? We know that the women must have said something to somebody because here we are today! Perhaps there is another explanation. Mark deliberately leaves the story open, pointing forward to the future, to the unfinished, to this moment, right here, right now, to the time beyond the point at which we encounter the text.

> We know that the women must have said something to somebody because here we are today!

The young man said to the women, 'Tell his disciples and Peter that he is going ahead of you to Galilee . . .' If we want to see the risen Christ then we need to go back to the beginning of Mark, where Jesus came to Galilee proclaiming the good news of God. Going to Galilee means reading the Gospel again, but this time with the light that is cast by the resurrection dawn, until we come once again to the journey towards the cross. Sometimes the complexities of our lives and of our relationships mean that we seem to go round in endless circles, but each time we learn something new. Sister Frances Dominica, the founder of Helen and Douglas House hospices in Oxford, speaks of valuing time in its depth rather than in its length, and so, standing at the empty tomb, the depth of feeling that the women experienced becomes tangible. Here we connect again with the importance of waiting, of being slowly attentive to the story. Not sitting around twiddling our thumbs; rather, waiting on God, which requires attentive, deep listening. After all, as we have seen, Mark starts his Gospel with a sense of urgency, with John the Baptist launching into a bold assertion that the time is *now*, the place is *here* and the purpose is *this*. And so Mark's Gospel ends not with a full stop but with a '. . .' – only this time, whatever happens next happens (so the Gospel tells us) in the light of the resurrection. The end is a beginning . . . the pilgrimage is a circular one, it keeps on going.

I fear that the role of the women at the end of Mark's Gospel has been frequently misrepresented and underplayed, when in fact they play a pivotal role, not least in the fact that Mark records them as being witnesses to the resurrection. He accords them the correct response of awe and wonder, not blind terror and weak withdrawal for the sake of fear; no, the women are not passive observers. Yet, as is so often the case, their role is articulated in the subtleties of the text (and the story): what is said, and what is left 'unsaid' . . .

Conclusion

One of the most significant archaeological discoveries of the twentieth century was the Dead Sea Scrolls. You may well be familiar with the remarkable story of their discovery, but perhaps less so with the controversy surrounding their dissemination to the general public (which rumbled on over a number of decades). In 1942 a young shepherd in Israel-Palestine was searching for a lost goat. Throwing stones resulted in the sound not of a bleating animal but of shattered pottery. Upon investigation, the shepherd stumbled across what turned out to be our earliest versions of the books of our Christian Old Testament (the Jewish Hebrew Bible). The ancient community that lived on the shores of the Dead Sea at a place called Qumran preserved and valued these books as the foundation of their Jewish faith. (Interestingly, however, they did not consider the book of Esther to be of value, the reason perhaps being that it does not once mention God.) I encountered the Dead Sea Scrolls as a graduate student in Oxford, and had the privilege of studying them with one of the scholars who was greatly involved with the struggle to make the scrolls 'public'. On one occasion my tutorial partner was ill, and so the task of translation and comment that week fell solely to me, a daunting prospect if ever there was one.

There was a problem, however, and it wasn't my laboured reading of the text. No, the problem was with the professor's glasses. Reading requires the ability to focus on the text and to see the script clearly. On this particular occasion a screw had come loose and a lens had fallen out. 'Can you fix this?' he asked me, and I was duly handed the glasses, the loose lens and the tiny screw that would hold it all together. Much to my relief, I was able to complete the (temporary) repair job, not a word more was said, and the tutorial proceeded. I look back on this incident now with much amusement, but given a predisposition to find meaning in the most trivial of incidents, I reflect not only on the matter of these ancient documents (particularly that they were disparate rather than collected together in one 'book', and that they contain many variations from the 'texts' we have today), but more on the manner of my encounter with them. The process of understanding came through translation (from Hebrew into English), but before even that could be attempted, the ability to focus in order to gain clarity had to be addressed. This is a process that should apply to all of us, whether we are short- or long-sighted, or neither!

In one sense, this book has invited us to engage with the texts of the Bible in a way that does not constrain them, holding on to their 'fundamental' importance, without being 'fundamentalist' in our reading. The many texts of the Bible urge us into being: to live, act, think and do, just as we are. The sort of Church that the Apostle Paul created, encountered and indeed wrestled with was a radical mix of rich and

> We need to hold on to the 'fundamental' importance of Bible texts, without being 'fundamentalist' in our reading

poor, young and old, male and female. But it wasn't put together overnight, and this can teach us a valuable lesson. In our reading together of the Bible, in our making sense of it, we are called into a deeper sense of engagement with God, one that combines our relatively brief time on earth with God's eternal nature. We all need time, therefore, to sustain and maintain our faith with one another, whether we are in agreement with each other or not.

If we start from the premise of a 'label', then that does not allow much room for manoeuvre. If we start from who we are (in relation to God), then that is less restricting, because any engagement with the text will make use of our God-given intelligence and imagination. This does not mean that any understanding will be overly domesticated or introspective. No, as Christians we live, move and have our being in relation to God the Trinity; our lives are interwoven with a God-shaped narrative. There has to be a connection between hermeneutics and theology (God-talk), between text and liturgy (work of the people), which is a collective expression of relationship, as the Bible is itself a collective expression of the God-shaped story that drives it, behind the text and in front of it. In order for the Bible to have meaning, it needs to be grounded in the missional life of the Church and the role that each and every child of God plays in it.

> For the Bible to have meaning, it needs to be grounded in the missional life of the Church

As I write this conclusion, I am reflecting on the well-travelled nature of this book. It began its life in the context of a conference group seeking to make sense of the Bible in the United Kingdom. Much of the book was written on the other side of the world, in Aotearoa New Zealand; and its finishing stages have been produced back where I started. Travel, of course, brings with it increasing perspective – indeed, how can it not? This is not to say that the preferred way of making sense of the Bible involves getting on an aeroplane and crossing oceans and continents; but making sense of the Bible might involve a journey of shifting interpretations, or seeing the texts from different angles, of allowing oneself to be transformed in ways that might challenge or unsettle.

As it happens, this idea of being challenged and unsettled is found in so many of the stories that the Bible contains. If we perhaps stop and ask whether our own lives make sense, and revel in the ways in which things that happen to us shape us and mark who we are, viewed from this perspective the Bible in all its complexities and confusions might speak in ways that allow meaning to be formed.

When we speak of the Bible as having 'authority', for my own part I have been far more influenced by models of authority that leave room for creativity, humility and growth, that foster and develop a vision that is firmly rooted, but which allows for the often unpredictable in-breaking ways of God. Christians are not called to 'seek, locate and destroy' (the classic cry of Doctor Who's enemy the Daleks), but rather surely to 'seek, locate and love' (let's call that the 'revisionist Dalek model'). I fail to see how the command to love one another can be truly held in combination with pointing one's finger at another person's particular 'sin' that needs to be repented of, because the Bible apparently says so: when and where and in what context? It seems to me that such approaches to the texts leave reason and intelligence outside the door, because if all we do is continually proof-text arguments, we are not engaging with our God-given intelligence.

The desk at which I type is part of the context in which I am rooted: an educational institution focused on training for ordination in the Church of England. It is an immense privilege and joy to journey with people who offer themselves for public ministry, and I have found my own identity as a priest and teacher changed and shaped quite profoundly through the encounters and conversations that I have shared with those under my care. Through those conversations we catch glimpses of the Divine, and encounter God in places even where the darkness can seem overwhelming. This has affected how I read, teach and preach on the texts of the Bible, and it is interesting how this 'daughter of the manse', brought up a firm Nonconformist, educated in a Church of England primary school and a Roman Catholic secondary school in the north-east of England followed by several years at university and degrees in biblical studies, has ended up where I am now. I say this, because it is important not to erode our own sense of the 'local' in how we search for meaning, and the many ways in which this 'local' might affect how we read the Bible. In my daily life I encounter the texts in a number of ways: in the lecture room, in the saying of the daily offices, in school assemblies, in the radio studio, in pastoral encounters, in preaching, and so on. Each context will raise different sets of questions about what a story might or might not mean, and whether a particular interpretation of a text is helpful or not.

Any encounter with the texts of the Bible should leave us changed, but not always in the ways we might expect. For me this is perhaps best summed up in the words of John Newton (1725–1807):

> I am not what I ought to be,
> I am not what I want to be,
> I am not what I hope to be,
> But by the grace of God
> I am not what I was.

Notes

———◆◆◆———

Introduction

1 'Hermeneutics' derives from the name of the Greek god Hermes, the messenger of the gods, and inventor of language and speech.

2 See in particular John Barton, *What is the Bible?* (London: SPCK, 2009).

3 I have heard it argued that the need for interpretation is itself a result of humanity's sinful nature, a 'tower of Babel'-like scattering of voices.

4 This frustration at the problems of relating academic study to other areas in which the Bible has relevance is shared by Sandra M. Schneiders' article 'Biblical Interpretation – the Soul of Theology' in *Australian Biblical Review* (Vol. 58, 2010, pp. 72–82). She writes, 'we will never get the Word of God under control, but if we remain in God's word by engaging it loyally with all the imagination and skill at our command, it will, as Jesus promised, increasingly lead us into the truth that will make us free' (see John 8.32) (p. 82).

5 The Wisdom tradition in the Old Testament includes the books of Proverbs and Ecclesiastes (an approach heralded by Richard Briggs in his books *Reading the Bible Wisely* (Grand Rapids, MI: Baker House, 2003) and *The Virtuous Reader: Old Testament Narrative and Interpretive Virtue* (Grand Rapids, MI: Baker Academic, 2010)).

6 Actually it can be very fruitful to acknowledge difference and discuss it constructively.

7 Interpretation itself needs to be ethical: 'our acts of interpretation are not ontologically different from our other acts' (A. K. M. Adam, *Faithful Interpretation: Reading the Bible in a Postmodern World*, Minneapolis: Fortress, 2006, p. 63). Difficulties arise when one line of interpretation is presented as 'correct' over and above all other actual or potential lines of interpretation. Having been present at several scholarly and ecclesiological 'shouting matches' I can vouch for the need for a more ethical approach to how we interpret the texts.

8 Justin Paton, *How to Look at a Painting* (Wellington, NZ: Awa Press, 2009), p. 80.

9 In the Jewish Babylonian Talmud (the sixth commentary on the Mishnah, which is itself a commentary on the Torah), it is written, 'No one can

understand the words of the Torah until he has stumbled over them'
(*bGit.* 43a). Commenting on this, Alexander Deeg writes: 'To be able to
stumble one must move closer to the text, pay attention to unevenness,
not resolve tensions too quickly, and discover with pleasure the gaps'
(from a lecture originally delivered on 22 November 2006 in Marburg,
Germany: 'Imagination and Meticulousness: *Haggadah* and *Halakhah* in
Judaism and Christian Preaching'; translated into English by Stephen
James Hamilton and presented at the Annual Meeting of the 'Academy
of Homiletic' in Boston, MA, 21 November 2008).

10 See John Barton, *How the Bible Came to Be* (London: Darton, Longman
& Todd, 1997).

11 The exhibition 'Brought Together' was on show in Christchurch Art Gallery,
Christchurch, Aotearoa New Zealand during the winter of 2010.

12 I am using the singular 'story' here quite deliberately. More is said about
the story/stories of the Bible in Chapter 1.

13 The need for a slow, patient reading of the Bible is advocated by Rowan
Williams in his article 'The Literal Sense of Scripture' in *Modern Theology*
(Vol. 7 No. 2, January 1991, pp. 121–34).

14 Paton, *How to Look at a Painting*, p. 29.

15 As explored in Walter Brueggemann's *Texts that Linger, Words that Explode:
Listening to Prophetic Voices* (Minneapolis: Fortress, 2000).

16 Rowan Williams, *Writing in the Dust: After September 11* (Grand Rapids,
MI: Eerdmans, 2002), p. 78.

17 Judith M. Lieu, *Christian Identity in the Jewish and Graeco-Roman World*
(Oxford: Oxford University Press, 2004), p. 372.

18 Paton, *How to Look at a Painting*, p. 59.

19 The need for an approach that is more critical and creative is not the
same as advocating pluralism. 'Anything goes' is different from saying that
'many paths should be given consideration'. The problem lies in placing
plural approaches in direct opposition to a singular line of interpretation,
a 'one or the other' way of thinking. It is more fruitful to focus on where
the points of difference lie and in reflection on what generates those differences. That is a far more open and honest approach, through which
we may learn more about ourselves and those with whom we disagree.
Jewish rabbinic discourse relies on multiple approaches being brought
together to focus on one text. Any points of difference are allowed to
remain in tension and in conversation with each other. Worth pursuing
is A. K. M. Adam's exploration of what he calls 'differential hermeneutics'
(*Faithful Interpretation*, pp. 81–103). If I understand his explanation of
this hermeneutical endeavour correctly then it is very similar to what

I have observed in Aotearoa New Zealand, particularly in the Anglican three-tikanga context: Maori, Polynesian and Pakeha, 'European'. 'Tikanga' can be translated as 'cultural stream'. Different context-based interpretations are constantly in respectful dialogue with one another. The difference between so-called 'integral hermeneutics' (where there is one correct interpretation) and 'differential hermeneutics' (which permits different approaches) centres on an ethical question: 'What sort of lives and interactions should our hermeneutics engender?' (*Faithful Interpretation*, p. 103).

20 A good place to start is with Letty M. Russell, *Just Hospitality: God's Welcome in a World of Difference* (Louisville, KY: Westminster John Knox, 2009).

21 Alan Jacobs, *Looking Before and After* (Grand Rapids, MI: Eerdmans, 2008).

22 Words I can attribute to Kwok Pui Lan from a session at the American Academy of Religions meeting in Montréal, November 2009.

23 A further observation about rainbows is that their points of origin and end look clear from a distance, but change according to the location of the observer.

24 Especially helpful is A. K. M. Adam's *Faithful Interpretation*. Adam argues that there is in fact no distinction between what the text *meant* and what it *means*. Interpretation is a continuous exercise (p. 28).

25 The interplay between theory and artistic practice is not a new enterprise. See in particular Rowan Williams, *Grace and Necessity: Reflections on Art and Love* (London: Continuum, 2005). David Kahan, in his article 'Bystander Theology and the Desire to End a Hermeneutic Hegemony' (*Biblical Theology Bulletin*, Vol. 40 No. 3, August 2010, pp. 138–47), observes that 'received tradition has been unable to access the text adequately, falling short of offering faith communities a suitable hermeneutic that decodes the world of Jesus' contemporaries' (p. 138). Kahan proceeds to introduce what he calls 'bystander theology', which turns to aesthetics, the fine arts, to develop exegetical and theological concepts that embody density, texture, and depth that elucidate how biblical persons can be understood today' (p. 138).

26 As found in the prayer book of the Anglican Church in Aotearoa New Zealand.

27 Adam, *Faithful Interpretation*, p. 100.

28 This is often described as the 'hermeneutical circle', or perhaps better still, the 'hermeneutical spiral', suggesting that understanding develops with each encounter that we have with the text. I wonder if the term 'hermeneutical koru' might be even more helpful? The koru, or unfolding fern frond, is representative of the life cycle, and symbolizes new growth. It

can often be found in the centre of crosses in Aotearoa New Zealand. In the same way as the church year progresses through the seasons, continually returning to the season of Advent, the start of the new church year, although we hear the heralding of Christ's birth again, we ourselves are not the same as we were the previous year. We bring to the encountering of these texts whatever we have experienced in the past year, anticipating the hope that the incarnation will bring, breathing new life into our own lives. The acknowledgement of my own ('present') context in writing is important and necessary, since my understanding of texts has been broadened through travel and through the experience of living (albeit temporarily) in another place. There is some merit to this if we accede to A. K. M. Adam's observation that 'one promising place to begin our inquiry into alternatives to modernity's hegemony is in the margins of modern biblical-theological discourse' (*Faithful Interpretation*, pp. 34–5), in places that aim to produce readings that go against the grain of patriarchalism and colonialism.

29 The art installation was Fiona Connor's entry to the Walters Prize, Auckland Art Gallery Toi o Tāmaki, 24 July–31 October 2010. Speaking about her work, the artist comments: 'when I make an exhibition I approach it as a one-off project. I work with systems that shape our reality to draw attention to them and demonstrate potential for transformation'. Connor won the people's choice award for her work.

30 Paton, *How to Look at a Painting*, p. 71.

1 Stories

1 As reported on the Durham Diocesan website: <www.durham.anglican.org/news-and-events/> (accessed 24 September 2010).

2 According to official Broadcasters' Audience Research Board information.

3 Rowan Williams, 'The Literal Sense of Scripture' in *Modern Theology* (Vol. 7 No. 2, January 1991, pp. 121–34). An excellent summary of how understanding genre can assist with meaning is found in Marshall D. Johnson, *Making Sense of the Bible: Literary Type as an Approach to Understanding* (Grand Rapids, MI: Eerdmans, 2002).

4 One example is the identification of a framework of sin–exile–restoration in the biblical narrative (otherwise known as 'the story of Israel'). While it claims that this may still allow for unity and diversity in the Bible, it remains elusive in its ability to truly make sense of the variety of stories contained in the Bible in ways that might be both helpful and meaningful beyond the somewhat enclosed interpretative arena of scholarship.

5 See Williams, 'The Literal Sense of Scripture', p. 133 note 7. Williams specifically understands 'taking time' in a sequential sense.

6 Williams, 'The Literal Sense of Scripture', p. 122.

7 See page 11.

8 This is precisely the approach advocated by Susan Gillingham in *The Image, the Depths and the Surface: Multivalent Approaches to Biblical Study* (Sheffield: Continuum, 2002). Part of the difficulty with the search for meaning (she reflects) is that there is often a divide between so-called pre- and post-modern approaches to the texts, between historical-critical study and literary-critical study. Gillingham seeks a way to allow both approaches to contribute to the discussion, a process she also discussed in her earlier book *One Bible, Many Voices: Different Approaches to Biblical Studies* (London: SPCK, 1998).

9 A. K. M. Adam, *Faithful Interpretation: Reading the Bible in a Postmodern World* (Minneapolis: Fortress, 2006), p. 103.

10 Christchurch Art Gallery, Aotearoa New Zealand.

11 Rowan Williams, *Anglican Identities* (Cambridge, MA: Cowley Publications, 2003), p. 75.

12 For a very useful and insightful summary of the issues see Gillingham, *One Bible, Many Voices*.

13 Some of the difficulties in interpreting the New Testament letters are discussed by L. William Countryman in *Interpreting the Truth: Changing the Paradigm of Biblical Studies* (New York: Trinity Press International, 2003), particularly p. 89 onwards.

14 N. T. Wright, 'How Can the Bible be Authoritative?' in *Vox Evangelica* (Vol. 21, 1991, pp. 7–32).

15 As discussed by A. K. M. Adam in *Faithful Interpretation*, p. 117.

16 An excellent (and helpfully brief) overview of the contents of the Bible may be found in John Barton, *How the Bible Came to Be* (Louisville, KY: Westminster John Knox, 1998), pp. 1–12.

17 'Exegesis' means critical interpretation of a text, deriving from the Greek word meaning 'to lead out'.

18 Walter Brueggemann, *The Bible Makes Sense* (Louisville, KY: Westminster John Knox, 2001), p. 15.

19 Williams, *Anglican Identities*, p. 123.

20 Chris Saines, Director of Auckland Art Gallery Toi o Tāmaki.

21 See the exhibition catalogue by Francis Pound, *Stories We Tell Ourselves* (Auckland: David Bateman, 1999). The exhibition, 'Stories We Tell Ourselves: The Paintings of Richard Killeen', was held at Auckland Art Gallery Toi o Tāmaki, 9 September–5 December 1999.

22 Brueggemann *The Bible Makes Sense*, pp. 23–31.

23 I am grateful for this insight gained in conversation with the Revd Dr Sue Patterson of Bishopdale Theological College in Nelson, Aotearoa New Zealand.

24 As reported by the British Press in October 2010.

25 Justin Paton, *How to Look at a Painting* (Wellington, NZ: Awa Press, 2009), p. 102.

26 David Kahan, 'Bystander Theology and the Desire to End a Hermeneutic Hegemony' in *Biblical Theology Bulletin* (Vol. 40 No. 3, August 2010, p. 143).

27 Richard Bauckham, *Jesus and the Eyewitnesses* (Grand Rapids, MI: Eerdmans, 2006).

28 See Barbara K. Lundblad, *Marking Time: Preaching Biblical Stories in Present Tense* (Nashville, TN: Abingdon Press, 2007).

29 The *Tomorrow* series is by John Marsden and is published by Pan Macmillan, Sydney.

30 Brueggemann, *The Bible Makes Sense*, p. 47.

31 Nicholas King, *The New Testament – Freshly Translated* (Stowmarket: Kevin Mayhew, 2004).

32 Kahan, 'Bystander Theology', p. 141.

33 Brueggemann, *The Bible Makes Sense*, p. viii.

34 James Cone, *God of the Oppressed* (New York: Seabury Press, 1975), p. 103.

35 See Richard Briggs and the idea of reading itself as a 'virtue' (above, 'Introduction', note 5).

36 Alan Jacobs, *Looking Before and After* (Grand Rapids, MI: Eerdmans), p. 80.

37 Jacobs, *Looking Before and After*, p. 33.

38 In 2005 the BBC produced a retelling of the Easter story on the streets of Manchester. This was followed in 2007 by a retelling of the Christmas story on the streets of Liverpool. What was particularly interesting about these events was the fact that the story unfolded over a number of hours and across the cities, drawing in onlookers along the way. Although it was not a straightforward telling of the stories (in the sense of reading from one version of the story in the Bible), it remained faithful to the texts and was clearly identifiable as the story of Jesus' death and resurrection, and Jesus' nativity.

39 Alan Jacobs recounts this in his book *Looking Before and After*, p. 74, quoting from Tom Shippey, *J. R. R. Tolkien: Author of the Century* (Boston, MA: Houghton Mifflin, 2000), p. 107.

40 Henry Miller, *Tropic of Cancer* (New York: Grove Press, 1961), p. 2.

41 Jacques Maritain, *Creative Intuition in Art and Poetry*, p. 127, quoted in Rowan Williams, *Grace and Necessity: Reflections on Art and Love* (London: Continuum, 2005), p. 26.

2 Contexts

1 This is the opening sentence of L. P. Hartley's novel *The Go-Between* (New York: New York Review Books Classics, 1953/1966; London: Penguin, 2000). It is also used for the title of David Lowenthal's book *The Past is a Foreign Country* (Cambridge: Cambridge University Press, 1985), which looks at the way people use historical material to support present interests (mostly Anglo-American), which the author is critical of.

2 Bruce J. Malina, *The New Testament World: Insights from Cultural Anthropology* (revised edition, Louisville, KY: Westminster John Knox, 1993), p. 184.

3 See Chapter 4 for further details and a worked example from Mark's Gospel that draws together and illustrates many of the points made in this book.

4 For example, the two main scholarly bodies that meet annually, the Society of Biblical Literature and the American Academy of Religion, used to hold joint meetings until a disagreement over the nature of their relationship, driven by a desire on the part of some to assert identity over and against 'religion', caused the bodies to hold their meetings apart. This division will end in 2011, however, when joint meetings resume in San Francisco.

5 See especially L. William Countryman, *Interpreting the Truth: Changing the Paradigm of Biblical Studies* (Harrisburg, PA: Trinity Press International, 2003).

6 This is explored in more depth in Chapter 4.

7 Taken from a lecture on 5 August 2010 in the Conference Centre, University of Auckland.

8 Quote taken from an interview with Neil MacGregor in 2010.

9 See pages 13–14. For an excellent overview of how to understand the genres of the Bible, see Marshall D. Johnson, *Making Sense of the Bible: Literary Type as an Approach to Understanding* (Grand Rapids, MI: Eerdmans, 2002).

10 In 2006 Fiji's military leader Frank Bainimarama overthrew the elected government and instigated military rule.

11 In 1973 Geza Vermes published his ground-breaking book *Jesus the Jew: A Historian's Reading of the Gospels* (London: Collins). In the field of Pauline studies, the 'new perspective' debate was fuelled by a desire to see Paul more within his Jewish context.

12 Although the Dead Sea Scrolls were discovered by Qumran in the Judaean desert in 1946, they were not made available to the 'public at large' until the early 1990s. The scrolls are highly significant for a number of reasons,

not least that they give us a valuable insight into a previously unknown sect within Judaism at the time of Jesus. Our earliest manuscript versions of the books of the Hebrew Bible (the Christian Old Testament) also come from Qumran, with the exception of the book of Esther which the fiercely religious Dead Sea community apparently did not copy as it does not once mention God in its narrative.

13 For example, Matthew's emphasis on Jesus' missionary strategy being to the 'lost sheep of the house of Israel' (10.6) seems to jar with the sentiment of 27.25 ('His blood be on us and our children!').

14 A. K. M. Adam, *Faithful Interpretation: Reading the Bible in a Postmodern World* (Minneapolis: Fortress, 2006), p. 58.

15 Bruce J. Malina, *The New Testament World: Insights from Cultural Anthropology* (Louisville, KY: Westminster John Knox, 1981, 2nd edition 1993); John H. Elliott, *Home for the Homeless: A Sociological Exegesis of 1 Peter* (London: SCM Press, 1981) and *What is Social-Scientific Criticism of the Bible?* (Minneapolis: Fortress, 1993). Philip F. Esler's own work in this area began with his study of Luke-Acts (*Community and Gospel in Luke-Acts*, SNTSMS 57, Cambridge: Cambridge University Press, 1987). Drawing on the work of sociologists such as Peter Berger and Thomas Luckman, particularly their 1966 book *The Social Construction of Reality* (Garden City, NY: Anchor Books), and *The Sacred Canopy* (Garden City, NY: Anchor Books, 1967), which applied the methodology of the former book to the field of religion, Esler argued that the author of Luke-Acts creates a 'symbolic universe' presenting Christianity as a faith with a definite past. Esler stresses that there are 'particular relationships' between Luke's theology and his social, political and religious setting.

16 For examples see in particular Malina, *The New Testament World*.

17 As outlined in some detail by Mark D. Nanos, 'The Social Context and Message of Galatians in View of Paul's Evil Eye Warning (Gal. 3:1)', available on <www.marknanos.com>.

18 Norman Gottwald, *The Tribes of Yahweh* (Maryknoll, NY: Orbis, 1979); Robert Carroll, *When Prophecy Failed* (London: SCM Press, 1979).

19 M. Daniel Carroll R. (ed.) *Rethinking Contexts, Rereading Texts: Contributions from the Social Sciences to Biblical Interpretation* (Sheffield: Sheffield Academic Press, 2000).

20 Alan Jacobs, *Looking Before and After* (Grand Rapids, MI: Eerdmans, 2008), p. 59. Paul's 'body' image is nuanced by the imagery presented in the letter to the Ephesians 4.16: '. . . from whom the whole body, joined and knit together by every ligament with which it is equipped, as each part is working properly . . .'

21 Philip F. Esler, 'Models in New Testament Interpretation: A Reply to David Horrell' in *Journal for the Study of the New Testament* (Vol. 78, 2000, pp. 107–13).

22 Identified as being 'differential hermeneutics' by A. K. M. Adam in *Faithful Interpretation*, pp. 81–103. The advantage of providing a place for disagreement in the interpretative process is that it prevents one meaning being dominant and encourages respectful listening to 'the other'.

23 See page 26.

24 A. K. M. Adam, *Faithful interpretation*, p. 58.

25 See, for example, H. Räisänen *et al.*, *Reading the Bible in the Global Village: Helsinki* (Atlanta, GA: Society of Biblical Literature, 2000); D. N. Premnath (ed.), *Border Crossings: Cross-Cultural Hermeneutics* (Maryknoll, NY: Orbis, 2007); Curtiss Paul DeYoung, *Coming Together in the 21ˢᵗ century: The Bible's Message in an Age of Diversity* (Valley Forge, PA: Judson Press, 2009). In this latter book, especially valuable is the 'group reflection–action guide' on pp. 182–207. See also Daniel Patte (ed.), *Global Bible Commentary* (Nashville, TN: Abingdon Press, 2004).

26 Louise J. Lawrence, *The Word in Place: Reading the New Testament in Contemporary Contexts* (London: SPCK, 2009), p. 12.

27 I am grateful to Professor Paul Trebilco of Otago University, Aotearoa New Zealand, for these insights.

3 Encounters

1 See Rowan Williams, *Grace and Necessity: Reflections on Art and Love* (London: Continuum, 2005), pp. 138–9. Williams comments: 'The "what" of what is known is not something that simply belongs to the given shape we begin with in our perception; it extends possibilities, or even, to use a question-begging word, *invites* response that will continue and reform its life, its specific energy.'

2 Another way of interpreting this unfolding progression of interpretation is in a musical sense: in particular, the work of the cognitive scientist Douglas R. Hofstadter, who describes consciousness as being 'fugal'. However we encounter a work of art (or a text) is bound to trigger a whole series of related questions and thought-patterns. Hofstadter's work is explored by Rowan Williams in *Grace and Necessity*, pp. 135ff.

3 BBC online News magazine, 23 September 2010.

4 The Manchester Passion in 2006 was a contemporary retelling of the last few hours of Jesus' life using popular music from various Mancunian bands; the Liverpool Nativity did the same with the story of Jesus' birth, on the streets of Liverpool.

5 Even with Dillon's straightforward presentation of the Gospel, one review commented that 'what overwhelms is the absolute relevance of these ancient stories to the contemporary scene. The simple clarity of the teaching of Jesus transcends specifics of time and place. The radical message of loving one's enemies has never sounded so revolutionary, straightforward, obvious and utterly sensible' (*The Scotsman*).

6 This forms the basis of rabbinic interpretation, which we shall explore in the next chapter.

7 London: SPCK, 2009.

8 Translated into English as G. Bornkamm *et al.* (eds.), *Tradition and Interpretation in Matthew* (London/Philadelphia: SCM Press/Westminster Press, 1963), pp. 52–7.

9 Williams, *Grace and Necessity*, p. 21.

4 Conversations

1 As reported in *The Times*, 23 July 2009.

2 Judges 19 tells the story of a Levite from Ephraim who went to Bethlehem to retrieve his wife who had run off to her father's house. On their return journey they stayed at Gibeah with another Ephraimite. During the night, men from the city sought to rape the Levite, who gave them his wife to assault instead. In the morning he found her dead and he cut her up into twelve pieces, which he sent throughout Israel demanding action. Commentators often point out that the woman has no voice and no name.

3 See page 9.

4 Zadie Smith, *On Beauty* (London: Penguin, 2005).

5 One response of the New Zealand church to the crisis within the Anglican Communion has been to hold a series of hermeneutical hui (*hui* being the Maori word for 'meeting'). Exponents of different viewpoints come together and share their thoughts on contentious texts. Tim Meadowcroft reflects on the whole process in his article 'When Hermeneutics is Not Enough' in *Anglican Taonga* (No. 34, Spring 2010, p. 30).

6 Walter Brueggemann, *Interpretation and Obedience: From Faithful Reading to Faithful Living* (Minneapolis: Fortress, 1991), p. 113.

7 Lorraine Cavanagh, *Making Sense of God's Love: Atonement and Redemption* (London: SPCK, 2011).

8 G. W. Buchanan, *To the Hebrews* (Anchor Bible Commentary, Garden City, NY: Doubleday, 1972). See also Philip S. Alexander, 'Midrash and the Gospels' in C. M. Tuckett (ed.), *Synoptic Studies: The Ampleforth Conferences of 1982 and 1983* (JSNTSup 7, Sheffield: JSOT Press, 1984, pp. 1–18).

9 'Halakhah' derives from the Hebrew word *halakh* which means 'going'. Halakhah is therefore the kind of exegesis and interpretation that relates to the goings on in life, to law, commands and prohibitions. 'Haggadah' is everything else, the word being derived from the root *ngd* meaning 'to tell' or 'to narrate'.

10 The first letter of the word 'blessing' is also a 'b' (*berekah*). *Genesis Rabbah* is dated to the period of rabbinic interpretation between the years 400 and 600. See H. L. Strack and G. Stemberger, *Introduction to the Talmud and Midrash* (trans. Markus Bockmuehl, 2nd edition, Edinburgh: T & T Clark, 1996).

11 See above, 'Introduction', note 9.

12 Talmud Menachot 29a. Betty Rojtman, in *Black Fire on White Fire: An Essay on Jewish Hermeneutics, from Midrash to Kabbalah* (trans. Steven Rendall, Berkeley, CA: University of California Press, 1998), uses the tools of contemporary semiotic theory to analyse rabbinic hermeneutics, discovering what she argues is a striking modernity in these early forms of textual interpretation. She argues that there is a double-layered meaning to rabbinic exegesis that refers both to its own world and to the transcendent and eternal presence of God.

13 See Strack and Stemberger, *Introduction to the Talmud and Midrash*.

14 David Stern, *Parables in Midrash: Narrative and Exegesis in Rabbinic Literature* (Cambridge, MA: Harvard University Press, 1991), p. 6.

15 Daniel Boyarin, in a review essay of Stern's book, *Association of Jewish Studies Review* (Cambridge: Cambridge University Press, Vol. 20, 1995, p. 130).

16 A point made by J. D. Crossan in his work on the 'historical Jesus' and parables. This rather suggests the type of epic storytelling known to many cultures, and rather less so nowadays in popular Western tradition.

17 Barbara K. Lundblad, *Marking Time: Preaching Biblical Stories in Present Tense* (Nashville, TN: Abingdon Press, 2007).

18 Lundblad, *Marking Time*, p. 73.

19 Lundblad, *Marking Time*, p. 74.

20 A version of this textual example was published in *Modern Believing: Church and Society* (Vol. 51 No. 1, January 2010, pp. 37–43).

21 Christopher Rowland, *Christian Origins* (2nd edition, London: SPCK, 2002), p. 86.

Further reading

John Barton, *What is the Bible?*, 3rd edition, London: SPCK, 2009.

Paula Gooder, *Searching for Meaning: An Introduction to Interpreting the New Testament*, London: SPCK, 2008.

Alan Jacobs, *Looking Before and After: Testimony and the Christian Life*, Grand Rapids, MI: Eerdmans, 2008.

Christopher Rowland and Jonathan Roberts, *The Bible for Sinners: Interpretation in the Present Time*, London: SPCK, 2008.